T0354630

THE CALLING FROM GOD

MANY ARE CALLED, BUT FEW ARE CHOSEN

Dr. Lowell Hardy

WESTBOW
P R E S S®
A DIVISION OF THOMAS NELSON
& ZONDERVAN

"Scripture quotations are from the ESV® Bible (The Holy Bible, English Standard Version®), copyright © 2001 by Crossway, a publishing ministry of Good News Publishers. Used by permission. All rights reserved."

Scripture taken from the King James Version of the Bible.

WestBow Press books may be ordered through booksellers or by contacting:

WestBow Press
A Division of Thomas Nelson & Zondervan
1663 Liberty Drive
Bloomington, IN 47403
www.westbowpress.com
1 (866) 928-1240

ISBN: 978-1-9736-2131-7 (sc)
ISBN: 978-1-9736-2129-4 (hc)
ISBN: 978-1-9736-2130-0 (e)

Library of Congress Control Number: 2018905387

Print information available on the last page.

WestBow Press rev. date: 05/03/2018

For many are called, but few are chosen.
—Matthew 22:14

How shall they believe in him of whom they have not
heard? And how shall they hear without a preacher?
—Romans 10:14

CONTENTS

Homiletics Lectures 63

ACKNOWLEDGMENTS

My thanks and sincere appreciation are extended to the late Donald Millholland, PhD, my theological father and a theology professor at Shaw University Divinity School, for his invaluable advice and encouragement in the writing of this manuscript.

I am also indebted to Dr. Joseph C. Paige, Dr. Frank B. Weaver, Dr. Sandie Gravett, and Dr. James E. Arnette for grooming me for this task.

A very special thank-you to my wife, Portia, whose interest in this manuscript from its inception has been a source of encouragement and hope. Also, I am deeply indebted to my sister, Dianne, for the heart to take on the awesome task of typing this manuscript for me.

Finally, I must thank God and the Lord Jesus Christ, who have given me the mental, physical, and spiritual strength to endure the task of writing this manuscript, with the hope that others may be encouraged to answer the call to proclaim God's Word. "For without me ye can do nothing" (John 15:5). Thank you, Lord!

INTRODUCTION

The gifts of ministry are many, both specific and focused. In our modern age, the minister must have the ability to speak, teach, and administer; to possess the gift of compassion and concern for the needs of others; to exercise the gift of discernment and judgment; and to demonstrate the ability to heal by prayer, empathy, and comfort. Not all ministers possess gifts in equal measure, but preachers will likely be most effective if their best gifts can be identified and developed to the fullest. In other words, not all who seek to minister are endowed with effective skills for ministry.

Therefore, when we look at the call to preach, it is not simply an occupation for which individuals are recruited, regardless of how gifted they may be. One can possess great ability in the use of language, have a keen intellect, exhibit personal piety and godly behavior, and even demonstrate a strong desire to preach. But one thing is needed. In the same way that a regenerated heart is required for true membership in the church, a minister must experience something that can only be properly described as a divine call to that service: "And no man taketh this honour unto himself, but he that is called of God, as was Aaron" (Heb. 5:4).

The true nature of the call to preach is often a mystery to those who are called. At times, God's choices even seem unsuitable by human standards. The result of it is more certain, however, for those who are called approach the work of ministry from a deep, abiding, and unalterable conviction that such is the will of God for them. Those who are called exhibit the mark of the Holy Spirit upon their souls. Those called may freely state that they might have preferred a different work, one that might have brought greater wealth, more excitement, or greater recognition, but they could not make such a choice. Those called are not required to confess that there is nothing else they could do. Rather, they are called to confess that there is nothing else, by the grace of God, that they would do.

The exact nature of a call is impossible to describe fully, but there is nevertheless a pattern in the experience of those who are called: (1) The ones being called may experience the presence of the Holy Spirit wrestling with them, demanding, coercing, and cajoling a new perspective about God's will for them. (2) The ones who are called may remember a sacred moment or a holy place, like Jacob, who responded by saying, "Surely the Lord is in this place; and I knew it not" (Gen. 28:16). (3) The call can seem sudden, like the young Samuel being awakened from his sleep by the Lord, finally to respond, "Speak; for thy servant heareth" (1 Sam. 3:10). (4) Calls are experienced in great and dramatic episodes, as when Isaiah had a vision of the Lord on his throne surrounded by seraphims, and "heard the voice of the Lord, saying, Whom shall I send, and who will go for us?" Isaiah responded dramatically by saying, "Here am I; send me" (Isa. 6:1–8). (5) The call may also follow a time of quiet reflection. In fact, even dramatic calls are often preceded by lengthy periods of reflection and prayer. But the calling in any form lays a heavenly claim upon an earthly service in an unmistakable way.

Ministers respond to calls in different ways: (1) The response may be instantaneous and decisive, never to be raised for evaluation or question again. (2) For others, the response may be slow and prolonged, as other directions and purposes of life are tested and tried; yet the Spirit's urging returns to call them back from other purposes and plans. (3) For some, testing the call is, as with Jeremiah, a lifelong exercise of reevaluation and even a testimony with God. Such persons may return time and again to complain bitterly on their knees, saying, "O Lord, thou hast deceived me, and I was deceived: thou art stronger than I, and thou hast prevailed: I am in derision daily, everyone market me" (Jer. 20:7). (4) For still others, the call to serve God may come in the midst of lives and careers already in progress, as with the disciples who were called from their labors and professions. (5) Or, it may cause an almost complete reorienting of values and purposes, as with Paul on the Damascus road (Acts 9:1–22). (6) It may even come to lives that, until that moment, exhibited little to encourage one to think God could make use of them, as was the case with both Peter and Paul. Those who experience a call come to a recognition that the hand of the Lord is upon them and a response is required. (7) The strongest call seems to come to those who seem most likely to resist. But as individuals wrestle with the Spirit, as conviction works slowly in the soul, new insights emerge, new directions take shape, and new dreams are ignited. (8) Last but not least, the evidence of response can be found in the certainty of a conviction to serve, in the presence of a mind and spirit to discern the truth of the gospel and to make it clear to others, and in a desire to become qualified to serve in a way the Lord has called.

The call brings opportunities and responsibilities. Only those who are called are true candidates for effective preaching. The church has a responsibility to be a partner with them in acquiring the training, qualifications, and experience by which their gifts may be made suitable for God's work.

PART 1

THE CALL TO PREACH

INTRODUCTION

To promote the highest ends of the ministry, servants of God must begin with themselves. A ministry that is uncertain of its own power is a travesty of the sacred calling. Preachers are first of all humans who are answering the call of God. It is easy to pamper oneself and forget that the messenger is important, along with the message and methods. One may be like Apollos, "An eloquent man, and mighty in the scriptures," yet deficient to an extent in the way of God (Acts 18:24–26). Or such a person may be exercising a ministry like Thomas Chalmers of Scotland, "with a form of godliness, but denying the power thereof," or like John Wesley, waiting for that experience of the "warmed heart."[1]

In the fast pace of today, we are in danger of losing our souls and the knowledge of the secret known by Paul: "For to me to live is Christ, and to die is gain" (Phil. 1:21). The routine of day-to-day living may bring us to the verge of perfunctory automatism, and the call of the Spirit may seem faint and far away. But we should be sure of "the call from God," which carries us into the ministry of the Word.

Have we a sense of vocation? Without it, individuals will enter the sacred profession to their peril. Jeremiah 23:21–22 says, "I have not sent these prophets, yet they ran: I have not spoken to them, yet they prophesied. But if they had stood in

3

my counsel, and had caused my people to hear my words, then they should have turned them from their evil way, and from the evil of their doings." Hence, being in Christ before being in the ministry is foundational and indispensable. How can we be a blessing to others unless we ourselves are monuments of God's sovereign grace?

There is a natural religion and there is a revealed religion, but the only soul-saving religion is the religion of personal and spiritual experience. Paul speaks of being separated and called by the grace of God, who revealed his Son in Paul (Gal. 1:15–16). Therefore, the science of personal religion, the science of the inward spiritual life, is by far the most important, the most universal, the oldest, and the most fruitful of all the experimental sciences. The deeper the search into the Holy Scriptures, the more we discover ourselves in our sinfulness and in God's salvation for us. Paul said it well to Timothy: "Take heed unto thyself, and unto the doctrine; continue in them: for in doing this thou shalt both save thyself, and them that hear thee" (1 Tim. 4:16). The "here am I; send me" of Isaiah 6:1 followed a sense of the divine majesty and glory when the prophet knew the compelling love of God, and he could do nothing else other than respond.

Let no one at any time think of a better living than the call to preach, but only of a holier life. A sincere and right intention is necessary as the chief inducement to enter the function of the holy ministry. We need to watch our souls lest we are undone in the realm of motive. Even Moses, Jeremiah, Isaiah, Peter, and Paul feared to answer except by divine compulsion. Charles Haddon Spurgeon used to say that no person should enter the ministry who could keep out of it.[2] Preaching must become a passion, and ministry a sacred calling, or else it will be a very humdrum affair and a soul-destroying experience.

The Bible has plenty examples of the calling from God. Further illustrations of the call experience are found in the lives of J. Hudson Taylor, Samuel Rutherford, Dwight L. Moody, and Dr. Martin Lloyd-Jones, to name just a few. The power of the preacher and the preaching lies in the depth of the preacher's spiritual life. No one can really proclaim the mystery of the gospel unless he or she understands the significance of the divine revelation. It is noticeable that God chooses people who are busy—occupied with some kind of calling in life. The following list is by no means exhaustive.

1. Amos from the flock (Amos 7:14–15).
2. Moses from the flock (Exod. 3).
3. Gideon from threshing wheat (Judg. 6:11).
4. Deborah, who judged Israel (Judg. 4:4).
5. Samuel from ministering to Eli (1 Sam. 2:18–36).
6. Saul while hunting his father's mules (1 Sam. 9).
7. David from the flock (1 Sam. 16).
8. Jeroboam from rulership over the house of Joseph (1 Kings 11:28– 40).
9. Elisha from plowing (1 Kings 19:19).
10. Nehemiah while serving his king as a cupbearer (Neh. 1:11, 2 : 10).
11. Daniel while serving as a eunuch in the palace of Nebuchadnezzar (Dan. 1:19).
12. Peter and Andrew from fishing (Matt. 4:18–20).
13. John and James from fishing (Matt. 4:21–22).
14. Matthew from the tax office (Matt. 9:9).
15. Paul from hunting and persecuting saints (Acts 9:1–25).

Preaching as a method has probably been laughed at in a world given over to "power politics" and "earthly wisdom," but a true understanding of the "foolishness of preaching" (1 Cor.

1:17–31) is the only adequate way out of the present marshy ground of human despair and hopelessness. The well-known verse from Paul to the Corinthians in 1 Corinthians 1:18 is not an admission that preaching as a way of speaking is vanity and folly; rather, Paul is speaking to glorying in the power of the paradox—"the sheer folly of the Christian message." The Greek word is *kerygma*, the thing preached, and it was that which challenged the thinking and wisdom and religion of humankind then—and challenges them now. This central affirmation is none other than the focusing of the gospel in the redemptive passion of our Lord and Savior, Jesus Christ (Acts 1:3). Therein is judgment upon sin, sacrificial salvation, the cross, the resurrection, and always the enthroned eternal one active throughout the ages. From the scandal of the cross issues the glory of the gospel.

Every age in history has witnessed a breaking in by God's Spirit in the measure of the emphasis of this heartfelt message. It is expected that each person will proclaim with emphasis the gospel in his or her own accentuated way. Concentration upon the immortal themes will bring richness of knowledge and power to touch people's heartstrings. That which will save an individual from the sin of evasion of essential truth is that heartfelt passion for the gospel already experienced in personal life. A worker should step back at times to look at his or her call to preach. But the one to be pitied most is the person who has no regard for the high calling from God.

The true preacher is one who does not preach about things. Preachers should preach out of the fullness of things because they live at the heart of truth. As ministers of the Word, we must eliminate the possibility of failure—the ultimate necessity is the summoning of the mind and will to do our duty of handling the Word of God without any deceit or evasion. We may well rise up these days to greater things and leave behind the lesser things. With such a vision of the ruling Christ, whose gospel we proclaim as his ambassadors, we need not lose heart.

The preacher is summoned to a high calling and must match it with a high ethical character. Learn by the grace of God to walk worthy of the vocation wherein you are called. The preacher, more than any other vocation of people on earth, is under bonds to live nobly. The lawyer, when admitted to the bar, does not promise to keep the Ten Commandments. The physician, when receiving a degree, does not agree to live according to the principles of the Sermon on the Mount. The merchants and manufacturers do not profess to stand ready to give their lives for the ransom of others. But ministers who stand to proclaim the gospel in the pulpit or elsewhere, as ambassadors of Christ, undertake all this when they venture to address their fellow men and women for their moral shortcomings, or to make it clear beyond a peradventure that they are walking in the way of Jesus with honest hearts. If preachers preach to other people about how to live with any sort of efficacy, then they must do a lot of holy living themselves—and do it first to effectively proclaim the gospel of truth.

D. L. Moody would say that character is what a person is in the dark. It is what a person is when no human eyes are around, when all restraints are taken away. It is what the mind thinks when it is free to go where it likes and not where it must. It is what the heart desires in its secret longings and yearnings. It is what the person would really like to do, if he or she dared.[3] Unless your own essential person preaches the gospel of righteousness, peace, and joy, all your other preachments will become a mere beating in the air.

Once the call to preach is accepted, there is no excuse for anyone falling short at this point. It did not please the Lord to make a Horace Bushnell or a Henry Ward Beecher or a Phillips Brooks when he made all of us. Those men were possessed of rare and surpassing gifts. Each of them probably was given many talents, when in the same general distribution maybe some of us came in far less. But not one of these men had more direct access to God than is possible to any one of us. The supply of that grace, which gives insight and sympathy, fidelity and patience, courage and devotion, is as open and inexhaustible for us as it was for them. If you, with whatever measure of gifts God may have blessed you with, are bent on bringing those gifts up to their best by an earnest, consecrated use of them in seeking your fellows to those spiritual realities that you have experienced, then your ministry or call to preach will be splendidly fruitful.

All that has been said up this point was intended to point to a vital element necessary for the call to preach. That is, a person must be sanctified for the office even as Aaron was. Exodus 29:44 states, "And I will sanctify the tabernacle of the congregation, and the altar: I will sanctify also both Aaron and his sons, to minister to me in the priest's office." Sanctification here means to be set apart for a sacred purpose. It is the Greek word *hagiasmos*—a separation unto God from a profane, secular, and carnal use to a sacred, religious, and spiritual use. Sin is not necessarily involved in sanctification, because the word means setting apart. If sin is not involved in the person or material thing (e.g., the altar) set apart, then no sin is cleansed in the process of setting apart, but if sin is involved in a person or a material thing to be set apart unto God, then such must be dealt with to make it presentable to him.[4]

THE PEOPLE OF GOD

The concept of setting apart the people of God is threaded through both the Old and New Testaments. At the heart of it is the idea of a covenant that God made with a particular people. Why he selected the Hebrews is a mystery that the magnitude of his love alone will explain. The purpose of this choice is clear, however. This people would assist him in the reconciliation of humankind.

The covenant has two sides. On one side, it entails the promise of a continuing special relationship with God; on the other, it involves a responsibility. We may see both dimensions in different contexts in the history of the chosen people. To Abraham, God promised to make a great nation in him so that "all families of the earth be blessed" (Gen. 12:3). Through Moses, he reiterated the promise, saying, "If you will obey my voice indeed, and keep my covenant, then ye shall be a peculiar treasure unto me above all people: for all the earth is mine: And ye shall be unto me a kingdom of priests and a holy nation" (Exod. 19:5–6). Through the prophets, he repeatedly remonstrated with his people when they emphasized privilege and forgot their responsibility. According to Jeremiah, failure to fulfill their covenant obligation caused God to propose a new covenant—one unlike the one they broke so often. This one he would write in "their hearts" rather than on stone tablets. Thus, none would have to teach a neighbor about God, "for they shall all know me, from the least of them to the greatest, saith the Lord: for I will forgive their iniquity, and I will remember their sin no more" (Jer. 31:34).

Early Christianity took these thoughts and applied them to the church. They were not a new people but the same people, Israel, under a new covenant. What had applied to Israel, according to the Spirit, now applied to the church. Peter echoed the words of exodus when he spoke of the church: "But you are a chosen race, a royal priesthood, a *holy nation*, a peculiar people; that ye should shew forth the praises of him who hath *called* you out of darkness into his marvelous light" (1 Pet. 2:9; emphases mine). Note here that the new covenant entailed no change of purpose for the people of God. Newness had to do with inwardness and directness in the relationship between God and people. The mission of the people as a royal priesthood and a holy nation continued.

What could this calling entail? In ancient Israel, one of the purposes of priests was to keep the covenant relationship strong and vibrant. Thus, sacrifices symbolized renewal of the covenant relationship.

The phrase "holy nation" says something about the way in which the people were to carry out their reconciling mission to the nations. They could bear witness to a holy God by exemplifying his character in their own lives and in their society. As God is set apart from "the gods," so should his people be set apart from other peoples. Therefore, they would make God's name great by embodying love and justice in their lives together as his people.

UNDERSTANDING THE CALL

All of God's people are called, and all are called to ministry. Alongside this is the biblical recognition that some are called to ministry (called to preach) in a special sense beyond the call common to all God's people. The latter are sometimes referred to as the "equipping ministers," their calling being to prepare all "the saints" for the work of ministry (Eph. 4:12). This idea is prevalent throughout the Bible, and the two ways in which the term is used may be illustrated from 1 Corinthians 1:1–2, where Paul introduces himself as a "called apostle" and addresses the Corinthians as "called saints." In each usage, *called* is an adjective, not a verb. Paul was an apostle by divine calling, and all saints are God's people by calling (Rom. 1:1, 6–8; Rom. 8:28; Jude 1). That all God's people are called is explicitly stated in 1 Corinthians 7:17: "But as God hath distributed to every man, as the Lord hath called every one, so let him walk." The Greek noun here is *klesis*, which may be rendered as calling or vocation in Christ, for we are all called both to salvation and servanthood in Christ (1 Cor. 7:20; Eph. 1:18; Eph. 4:1, 4; Phil. 3:14; 2 Thess. 1:11; 2 Tim. 1:9; Heb. 3:1; 2 Pet. 1:10). Beyond the basic call common to all of us is the call that comes to some men and women to some specific ministry.

With the exception of Matthew 22:14, "calling" and "election" apply to the same persons (2 Pet. 1:10; Rev. 17:14).

God's people are his calling or election, two ways of describing the same thing. Emphasis may fall upon the act of divine calling or upon the resultant status. Matthew uses the term *called* for the invitation that goes out to all people, with some responding and some rejecting. He limits the term *election* to those who respond positively. On the parable of the marriage feast (Matt. 22:11–14), he concludes accordingly, "For many are called, but few are chosen." Context makes usage clear. God invites people of all kinds to his banquet, but the invited have the option of accepting or rejecting. Subsequently, they must live with the result. In other places in the New Testament, both terms apply to those responding positively.

Like calling, election implies God's initiative in our salvation and vocation. This excludes all boasting except in God, without whose call there could be no answer. It also excludes any excuse to those rejecting God's initiative. God's calling can be resisted, whether the call to discipleship extended to all people or the call to some special ministry extended selectively. God's grace is not irresistible. Jesus, saddened over Jerusalem, said, "O Jerusalem, Jerusalem, thou that killest the prophets, and stonest them which are sent unto thee, how often would I have gathered thy children together, even as a hen gathereth her chickens under her wings, and ye would not!" (Matt. 23:37). Many resist and then respond later. Resisting the call to ministry may grow out of the unwillingness to serve, as in the case of Jonah. Yet sometimes it relates to one's sense of unworthiness or inadequacy, as in the (temporary) case of Moses. God does not give up on us, but we may give up on him, whatever the motive for doing so. Of course, to reject God's calling is to ultimately deprive oneself of the fullness of life God wills for that person, to say nothing of depriving the many who otherwise would be served.

Election does not imply that God determined that some be saved and others lost. Our Lord puts the matter into focus: "Ye have not chosen me, but I have chosen you" (John 15:16). The verb here is *elect*. This does not imply coercion or that we have no choice; rather, the point is that ours is a response to his initiative. He sought us before we sought him. We are able to choose him only because he has already chosen us. Parallel ideas appear as to knowledge and love. We know God because He first knew us (Gal. 4:9). We love because He first loved us (1 John 4:10). It is in this sense that *election* is to be understood. Again, all of us are God's chosen or elected people. You are an elect race, a priestly kingdom, a holy nation, a people of God's own possession in order that you might proclaim the mighty deeds of the one who called you out of darkness into the marvelous light (1 Pet. 2:9). Election speaks of God's goodness, not partiality (Rom. 2:11). The opposite of election is not nonelection but disobedience.

CALLING IN THE RESTRICTIVE SENSE

Beyond the calling common to all God's people is his special calling of some as attested throughout the Bible, from people like Amos, the prophet of social righteousness; Hosea, the prophet of divine love; Moses and Huldah; and Elijah and Samuel to people like Peter and Philip's four daughters. This special calling is sometimes referred to as "called to full-time service," but this may be misleading. All God's people are called to full-time service. In his book *Vital Elements of Preaching*, Dr. Arthur S. Hoyt makes this arresting statement: "The Christian ministry is a calling that depends upon its vision of truth and life, and its sense of relation to them."[5] This author puts the minister's call first among the vital elements of his work. God has total claim upon us, and life is to be whole, not fragmented. This does not mean that all our time is to be spent in formal worship or service, but we are answerable to God for the whole of life. All life in Christ is to "labour therefore to enter into that rest," the Sabbath) (Heb. 4:11). The same principle holds for stewardship of money. Giving back a tithe (Old Testament) does not imply that the rest is ours to do with as we please. All we have belongs to God, and we are answerable to him for our stewardship of all of it.[6] This principle is mentioned because it applies to the calling that we have in common and the special calling limited to some. Both callings are full time, not part time.

Paid or unpaid (voluntary) are not decisive terms for distinguishing between calling in its general and special sense. In Judaism, the priests were paid in tithes and probably otherwise, but the prophets and scribes seem not to have received monetary compensation. Thus, some with a special call were paid, and some were not. Jesus and the twelve disciples received support from certain women who ministered to and with Jesus (Luke 8:1– 3). Paul recognized that "The laborer is worthy of his reward" (1 Tim. 5:18), yet he personally took pride in serving without pay. "For though I preach the gospel, I have nothing to glory of: for necessity is laid upon me; yea woe is unto me, if I preach not the gospel! What is my reward then? Verily that, when I preach the gospel, I may make the gospel of Christ without charge, that I abuse not my power in the gospel" (1 Cor. 9:16, 18). However, he did accept gifts and things from friends such as the Philippians (Phil. 4:15–18).

Baptist ministers have a long tradition in three patterns: (1) monetary support from those served, (2) service without pay, and (3) support from a third party as sponsor, whether church, convention, missionary society, or otherwise. Even the term *voluntary* does not distinguish between general and special calling. All of us are volunteers in the sense that God's calling does not coerce or override our freedom of response.

How do we really distinguish between the general calling common to all and the special calling that comes to only some? The mystery cannot be completely dispelled. For reasons known only to God, he seems to call some to be ministers in a sense not common to all his people. Both the Bible and continuing experience attest to this. God called Moses when he didn't call the thousands in Israel, even though they were his people whom he called.

Sometimes, individual gifts seem to account for God's choices of some for special ministries, but God also works in special ways through some "unlikely subjects." Just what the call is and how it comes are not always easy to explain. We know there is no fixed uniformity about it. The ways of God are not patterns by which every workman must be molded. His methods are as varied as the temperaments and dispositions of the individuals with whom he deals.

Certainly, the call does not come as an audible voice to everyone who enters the ministry. Perhaps it never comes in that way, yet we dare not limit God. There may be some who are stirred by a great, inescapable challenge as was Moses at Mount Horeb. For others, there is the still small voice that came to Elijah at the same Mount Horeb. It is probably never necessary for the man (or woman) who enters the ministry to rely upon such phenomena as exciting dreams or startling signs. We may be fairly confident, however, that no one should feel called to the gospel who does not have the overwhelming conviction that there is no other work on this earth equal to the ministry in its high and holy character and demands. There must be a passionate, impelling love for souls and lost souls, and the unceasing desire to give oneself to Christ without reserve. In such a commitment, there is no place for selfishness and personal ambition that the minister has not surrendered to the Lord. A minister's prayer should be like the one a great preacher uttered many years ago.

Oh, come, though mighty wind; come, Holy Spirit, and waft me onward and higher, and still higher, till my entire self shall be absorbed in the glory of the Son of Righteousness! Like Him, to be meek and lowly; like Him, to be crucified to the world; Like Him, if need be, crucified for the world; like Him, to weep for sinners; like Him to say, "Not my will, O Father, but thine be done." Oh! to have no thought but "Christ Crucified," to have no ambition but to win souls to heaven.[7]

However described or explained, God did call Moses, Deborah, Isaiah, Huldah, Jeremiah, Elijah, John the Baptist, the twelve, Philip's four daughters, Paul, and countless others in a sense that he has not called all his people particularly. This distinction is neither to be denied nor exaggerated.

EQUIPPING MINISTRIES

The distinction and relationship between calling to ministry in its general and specific sense is explicit in Ephesians. The Church as a whole, as the body of Christ, is the ministering body of Christ and is given various ministries for equipping all the saints for the work of ministry (Eph. 4:11–12). The overriding theme of Ephesians is God's eternal purpose to unite humankind, both Jew and Gentile, in Christ, "who hath made both one, and hath broken down the middle wall of partition between us" (2:14). God purposed "to make in himself of twain one new man, so making peace" (2:15). People once alienated from one another as Jew and Gentile that he "might reconcile both unto God in one body by the cross, having slain the enmity thereby" (2:16), thus creating one body in Christ.

Adding one analogy to another, Paul saw this "new creation" as "fellow citizens with the saints, of the household of God," "an holy temple in the Lord," and "an habitation of God through the Spirit" (Eph. 2:16–22). But Paul argues more than the oneness of God's people in Christ; he sees them as corporately the ministering body of Christ (Eph. 4:12–16; 1 Cor. 12:12–28; Rom. 12:4). Also, he recognizes certain ministries as special ones designed "for the equipping of the saints for the work of ministry" (Eph. 4:11–12). The whole Church is the ministering body of Christ, but there were also such special ministers as

18

apostles, prophets, evangelists, pastors and teachers who were given to the church to prepare all the saints for the work of ministry. A brief discussion will follow.

In a real sense, there is only one minister, the living Christ.[8] Jesus Christ is not dead but alive. He is not absent but present. He is not present just spiritually but embodied in the church, the body of Christ.[9] The living Christ is continuing his ministry through his church. The "body of Christ" is inclusive of all his people. Thus, all who belong to Christ participate in his continuing ministry. It is Christian ministry to the extent that Christ is the motivating force and power in ministry. Much goes on in the name of Christian ministry with which Jesus has nothing to do. The label does not always tell what's actually inside the package.

In its general or inclusive sense, Christian ministry occurs wherever or whenever we suffer and/or serve him in serving others. Jesus taught that in serving others, we serve him (Matt. 25:35–36). Paul dared even to see his suffering as a minister as the continuing suffering of Christ, "Who now rejoice in my sufferings for you, and fill up that which is behind of the afflictions of Christ in my flesh for his body's sake, which is the church" (Col. 1:24). All true followers of Christ minister in this sense.

Paul recognized a special ministry to and through the church. This is commonly known as the "equipping ministry" (Eph. 4:12). Just as the physical body needs to be conditioned and trained if it is to function competently, so must the church as the body of Christ be nourished, enlightened, disciplined, motivated, encouraged, and ministered to if it is to function competently in its ongoing ministry. This is the primary role of the equipping ministers. Of course, these equipping ministers serve in their own right. The role of equipping others does not exempt them from direct ministry to human need any more than guiding others in worship is a substitute for worship on the part of the worship leader. The equipping minister ministers directly also as a member of the body of Christ. The equipping minister models ministry, itself one significant way of equipping the saints for ministry. The equipping minister bears the burden of teaching, training, awakening, motivating, guiding, encouraging, and otherwise enabling "the saints" to find and fulfill their own calling as members of the body of Christ.

Paul, you will recall, identified the equipping ministers of the church as "apostles, prophets, evangelists, and pastors/teachers" (Eph. 4:11). Other lists appear elsewhere, not corresponding exactly to this list. Each list is apparently more illustrative than definitive (1 Cor. 12:4–11; Rom. 12:6–8). These ministers are given to the church of the living Christ—the very Christ who descended into the world and ascended into heaven "That he might fill all things" (Eph. 4:9–10). It appears here that Paul uses Psalm 68:18 as his text, adapts it to his need, and applies it to the continuing presence of Christ in his church, receiving gifts to equip his ministers. Ephesians 4:11 states, "And he *gave* some," whereas the term *gave* seemingly is used instead of *called*, as these are two aspects of the same larger reality. Christ calls such ministers to himself and to ministry; he gives them to the church as its equipping ministers.

Briefly, apostles were a unique group, with no successors.[10] Most scholars would agree. They first included only the twelve men who had accompanied Jesus from his earliest days to his ascension, and who were witnesses of his resurrection, and who were commissioned by him to the basic ministry of witnessing to his resurrection (Acts 1:21–22). Paul, although not a follower until after the resurrection, claimed to be an apostle on the grounds that he had seen the risen Lord and had been directly commissioned by him (see 1 Cor. 9:1). Apostles can have no successors because none of us has seen the Lord in the physical sense as these have. It may be noted, however, that many saw the risen Christ, up to five hundred at one time (1 Cor. 15:6), but only a few were commissioned (called) to be apostles.

Evangelists are those who tell the good news of what God has done and is doing to offer salvation to any who will receive it. This is the initial and basic ministry of calling all people to the faith and discipleship under Christ. Evangelism is ministry in which all Christians may have part, yet provision is made for the special ministry of those best equipped to lead and equip others in the work of evangelizing. Philip was an evangelist in this special sense (Acts 21:8). The ministry of evangelism as inclusive of "all the saints" and the ministry of evangelism in the special sense in which Philip was an evangelist are not competitive. This same ministry in two shapes illustrates what is true for all Christian ministry: it should include all the saints, but there is need and provision for special, equipping ministries.

Pastors and teachers seem to be joined, implying the ongoing nurturing of the saints. These terms are more serviceable in indicating directions than as definitive or exhaustive limits of the ministry in view here. In fact, this limited list of ministries gives only main lines and not the vast areas of human need requiring ministry. Again, although these imply various aspects of ministry, it does not follow that any minister is limited to only one ministry. A minister may preach, evangelize, serve as pastor, teach, and minister in many other ways. The passage does not indicate specific aspects of ministry, and it implies that the ministry may be weighed in a certain direction for a minister. One may be especially equipped for or devoted to preaching, teaching, or shepherding, or whatever God has deemed for the minister.

Prophets are preachers, proclaimers of the Word of God as they have heard it. Prophecy sometimes has to do with the future, but that is not its essence. A prophet is one who speaks for God to his people, proclaiming the heard word. This usage may be seen throughout scripture, as in Luke 1:67, where it is said, "And Zachariah, his father [father of John the Baptist], was filled with the Holy Spirit and prophesied, saying ..." What follows is preaching. I submit, then, that the one called to preach must be filled with the Holy Spirit (this will be discussed in detail later).

Peter defended his fellow disciples on the day of Pentecost of not being drunken babblers but as ones fulfilling what was foretold by the prophet Joel: "And your sons and your daughters shall prophesy" (Acts 2:17). Philip the evangelist had four daughters who prophesied—that is, preached (Acts 21:8–9). Thus, both men and women are known in the New Testament as prophets or preachers, just as is found in the Old Testament (Deborah, Huldah, and Isaiah's wife; more on these later). Romans 10:14–18 is a classic passage on preaching as proclaiming the "heard word." Paul makes a play on the Greek word *akoe* (as in "acoustic"). God's Word must first be a hearing before it can be a proclaiming. In Greek, *akoe* can be used for either. Not everything preached is Christian preaching. The living Christ is "the preacher," and only to the extent that we hear him can we preach him. In a sense, all the saints can hear and proclaim his word, but in the wisdom of God, provision is made for the special ministry of some who by virtue of personal gifts, background, or advantage are otherwise in a better position to hear and proclaim, or with no particular advantage but by the grace of God is called to preach.

SOME BIBLICAL EXAMPLES
OF CALLING

The fact of calling is more extensive in the Bible than the explicit employment of the term. That is most certain in biblical perspective and witness—the fact that God does single out some persons for special ministries. Sometimes the calling seems to be matched to one's personal gifts or background or preparation, but sometimes God seems to work through unlikely instruments. For example, a committee (pulpit or otherwise) would not necessarily have picked Joseph or David from among the children of Jacob or Jesse, respectively, but both Joseph and David proved to have gifts for the roles assigned to them. Furthermore, it is apparent from biblical witness that there is a wide range of ministries, and there is no stereotype in God's way of calling people into the ministry. A review of some who served God in special ways should reflect this variety in how God calls and to what He calls them to do.[11]

Prophetess

What exactly was a prophetess? The term was used to denote the wife of a prophet (Isa. 8:3). Possibly, she was endowed with the gift of prophecy. God had spoken to Isaiah that he should prophesy and write it in a scroll that he was to have a son by the prophetess, his wife, and that he should name the child Maher-shalal-hash-baz "For before the child should have knowledge to cry, My father, and my mother, the riches of Damascus and the spoil of Samaria shall be taken away before the king of Assyria" (Isa. 8:4). According to God's command, the prophecy was properly recorded before faithful witnesses who could affirm that the prophecy was given at a time it was declared by the prophet. This was done that Judah might believe it was of God. "And he shall pass through Judah; he shall overflow and go over, he shall reach even to the neck; and the stretching out of the wings shall fill the breadth of the land, O Immanuel" (Isa. 8:8).

The most noted of the prophetesses mentioned in the Bible were Miriam. It was because Miriam led the concert (Exod. 15:20, 21) that she was reckoned as a prophetess. Also, Deborah (Judg. 4:4), Huldah (2 Kings 22:14; 2 Chron. 34:22), Noadiah (Neh. 6:14), and Anna (Luke 2:36) were prophetesses. The four daughters of Philip (Acts 21:8, 9) are also said to have prophesied (probably meaning preached). It is probable that Miriam, Deborah, Huldah, and others were called prophetesses, not so much because they were supposed to be gifted with a knowledge of futurity, like the seers, but that they possessed a poetical inspiration—inspired (especially sacred) poetry being always deemed of supernatural and divine origin. Jezebel is mentioned as calling herself a prophetess (Rev. 2:20). There are false prophetesses and also false prophets who pretend to be inspired by God. Christ warns against such persons in Matthew 7:15.

Notwithstanding, God calls women to ministry. This is the clear witness of Old Testament and New Testament. Deborah was a prophetess, a judge, and a hymnodist. Here was a ministry of the Word of God, expressed in sermon, song, and counsel.

Her ministry was of great magnitude, having a major role in the deliverance of her people of Israel. There is no record of how her call came about, but that God did call her is the inescapable inference from her ministry (Judg. 4–5). From this story, we learn that what God does with a life is the validity of the call behind it, even where there was no burning bush!

Although remembered as the "Josiah Reforms," the dominant figure in the reforms around 640 BC was not king Josiah, the priest Hilkiah, or the secretary Shaphan, but rather Huldah the prophetess, a woman who "dwelt in Jerusalem in the college" (2 Kings 22:14). When the long-lost law was found in the temple, King Josiah recognized that the nation was in trouble because of its gross neglect of the (Mosaic) law. He called together Hilkiah the priest and the chief men in his cabinet and commanded them, "Go, inquire of the Lord for me, and for the people, and for all Judah, concerning the words of this book that has been found" (22:13). Hilkiah the priest and the chief men of the state went to Huldah the prophetess for guidance as to "the Word of the Lord."

Not a word is given as to Huldah's call to ministry. That she was a minister of the Word of God is explicit. Her validation as a minister is in the dominant role she played in responding to her nation's plea for help in a time of need. The ultimate test of ministry: "By their fruits you shall know them" (Matt. 7:16). As with Huldah, so with ministers today. The bottom line is the quality of life furthered by what is called ministry.

Ecstatic Prophecy

Samuel proclaimed the Word of the Lord to Saul, saying,

> Afterward you will come to the hill of God
> where the Philistine garrison is; and it shall be

> as soon as you have come there to the city, that you will meet a band of prophets coming down from the high place with harp, tambourine, flute, and lyre playing in front of them; they will be in a prophetic frenzy. Then the Spirit of the Lord will come mightily upon you, and you shall *prophesy* with them and be turned into another man. (1 Sam. 10:5–6)

The Hebrew word that is translated here as *prophesy** has a stronger meaning than what is given to that word. It means "to prophesy ecstatically." Usually we use the word *ecstasy* to describe an experience of being overcome with an emotion so powerful that self-control or reason may be suspended.

In this case, however, the ecstasy arises not from mere emotional rapture but from the Spirit (ruah) of the Lord, which falls upon a person, takes control of the center of the self, and makes them an instrument of the divine will. It is no wonder that Samuel promised that Saul would be turned into "another man"—no longer would he be just Saul the son of Kish, but Saul possessed by the Lord's Spirit! In such a prophetic state, unusual things happened, as we learn in another story that tells how Saul, again seized by prophetic ecstasy, stripped off his clothes and lay naked and stunned all day and all night (1 Sam. 19:19–24). These stories remind us of those Christians who, on the day of Pentecost, the Spirit was poured upon them, and men of Judea and Jerusalem thought they were drunken (Acts 2:1–13). Under the influence of the divine Spirit, the body was sometimes stimulated to hyperactivity, as in the case of Elijah,

---

* Note: the word *prophesy* comes from the Greek compound "to set or stand out," thus "to put out of place, derange, to be beside oneself."

who ran before the king's chariot with superhuman energy (1 Kings 18:46).

The Prophetic Preacher's Passion

It is a popular belief that the prophets of Israel were fierce and forbidding individuals, fiery and at times even ferocious in their stern attacks upon existing evil. This view is certainly justified on the basis of a study of the prophet's language. Their choice selection of pungent, arresting words and the emotional manner of the speeches are revealed in their writings. For example, Jeremiah cries out about the nation's scornful rejection of Israel's God, "My bowels, my bowels! I am pained at my very heart; my heart maketh a noise in me; I cannot hold my peace, because thou hast heard, O my soul, the sound of the trumpet, the alarm of war" (Jer. 4:19).

The prophetic mood was certainly not one of still waters flowing quietly through green pastures. The prophets were men of deep conviction and of strong passion. They found it impossible to mix words with logical nicety or to be dispassionately objective when they preached or delivered their oracles. They were supremely dedicated men, possessed men. Without this passion, the prophets would have ceased to be prophets, so characteristic was it of their lives and thoughts.

I hope to show the nature of this passion and possibly to determine its source, and its relation to the prophets' preaching. This passion appears to have had its origin in the initial call of the prophet. This crucial experience was evidently vividly remembered by the prophets Isaiah, Jeremiah, and Ezekiel. Others like Amos, Hosea, and Micah also seem to point to this experience, although the data are not so clear with respect to them. For some of the prophets, there is no dependable information on the matter of a call, although we may presuppose it in some cases. This phase of the prophet's life is particularly important, for it goes to the root of the prophetic preacher's motivation for their task. The call to prophesy is clearly parallel to the call to preach in the careers of present-day ministers. My aim is a simple one: the identification of the key features of the call experience. These clues will help in comprehending the dimensions of the prophet's devotion and should help those called to preach examine their dedication to their work as spokesman and proclaimer of the Word of God.

The prophets were convinced that they had been called by the God of Israel. They were certain that their prophetic careers were furthered by the active intervention of the Lord of history, the self-revealed redeemer of Israel. God had specifically summoned them to embark upon a career to prophecy to a stubborn nation. Amos explained his activity in Bethel by stating that the Lord had taken him from his work as herdsman and a gatherer of sycamore fruit to be his prophet, although he rejected the title of prophet for reasons noted. Amos was sensitive to national sins. He was grieved by the injustices under which the poor and underprivileged writhed. He was convinced that God would not suffer the rebellion of his people any longer, so he answered the divine summons and went to Bethel, and perhaps to Samaria. What else could he do? God's call was irresistible.

> The Lion has roared, who will not fear? The
> Lord God has spoken, who can but prophesy?
> (Amos 3:8)

The most eloquent of all prophets, the one from whom most can be learned as to preaching, is obviously Isaiah. He was a highly educated man, a man of refined taste, and a man

of singular literary power and skill. His writings take their
literary character from the natural endowments, educational
advantages, and social conditions of the man. The study of
Isaiah has educated many a preacher's imagination to the extent
that it seems he may not have been conscious of it, and few
things are as important to a preacher as the real cultivation of
imagination.[12]

Isaiah recounts how his call came when he was in the temple,
perhaps on the occasion of national mourning over the death of
Judah's king, Uzziah. "In the year that king Uzziah died I saw
also the Lord sitting upon a throne, high and lifted up, and his
train filled the temple" (Isa. 6:1). Here he was overcome with a
sense of the overwhelming holiness of God and had no answer
to give except to lament his unworthiness and uncleanness. But
when the direct question came from the Lord, "Whom shall I
send, and who will go for us?" He responded with the words,
"Here am I; send me" (Isa. 6:8). Awe, indecision, doubt, and
self-deprecation were banished when Isaiah sensed the glorious
and commanding majesty of the God who called him. As a
leading citizen in Jerusalem and a relative of the royal family,
Isaiah was conscious of the ominous rise of the power of mighty
Assyria and of its threat to Judah's security and independence[13]
God initiated the call to ministry, but Isaiah heard the call in the
context of need, his own and that of his people. Not every call
comes in this way, but this is one way in which it came. The
two key ingredients here are the awareness of human need and
of God's sovereign will to meet the need.

Next, there was Micah, a peasant farmer; a rugged, bold,
forthright champion of the oppressed; and opponent of the
trend toward larger farms; and a foe of absentee landlords (Mic.
2:2). His was a holy anger against the pseudo-religionists who
championed nothing except the satisfaction of their appetites.

29

He loosed a righteous wrath against the nation's insensitivity to widespread evil. It was a supernatural wrath, which Micah was compelled to identify with God, acting in him.

> But truly I am full of the power by the spirit
> of the Lord, and of judgment, and of might,
> to declare unto Jacob his transgression, and to
> Israel his sin. (Micah 3:8)

God had called him, directed him in his course, and empowered him to be a prophet. To God's purposes, the prophet was passionately committed.

And there was Hosea, distraught by the gross sensuality that flaunted itself as a religion. To him, there came with clarity the divine command to act by entering into a monstrous marriage. Hosea demonstrated in his life and in his words his protest against the nation's idolatrous licentiousness and his own dedication to the one God of righteous love. "Then said the Lord unto me, Go yet, love a woman beloved of her friend, yet an adulteress, according to the love of the Lord toward the children of Israel, who look to other gods, and love flagons of wine" (Hosea 3:1).

Probably the youngest of them all when the call came was Jeremiah. The Lord called him when he was about eighteen years old. Jeremiah protested that he knew not how to speak, being only a youth (Jer. 1:6). This great prophet was anything but a volunteer. But the Word of the Lord came to him to the effect that God had chosen him from before his birth and "ordained thee a prophet to the nations" (1:5). He began a career that was so fraught with pain and sorrow and frustration that men compared Jeremiah with the man of Galilee. No prophet has been assigned a more thankless task than Jeremiah, whose lot it was to call his nation to realities it did not want to face.

There were times when the burden of preaching with integrity was so crushing that Jeremiah begged for release (20:7–18), and he never became completely reconciled to his calling. In fact, Jeremiah felt that God called him to minister at the point not of his strength but of his weakness. Jeremiah is not a typical minister, but many ministers identify with him. But along with the yearning for release was Jeremiah's inner compulsion to preach. *"His word was in mine heart as a burning fire* shut up in my bones, and I was weary with forbearing, and *I could not stay"* (20:9; emphasis added). Not every minister is caught up in such an ordeal as Jeremiah, shrinking back from a thankless task and yet finding no release from it. Jeremiah preached because he could not silence within him a word from God, a word that he gladly would have left to some other proclaimer.

After Judas betrayed his call to ministry (Acts 1:17), the early Church sought a replacement for him among the twelve. Praying for God's guidance, they nominated two men and then sought further guidance for the final choice. This is not a pattern normally followed, but this is how Matthias came to be "enrolled with the eleven apostles" (1:26). There have been other examples in which a congregation took the initiative in calling someone into the ministry. Notable examples among Southern Baptists are George W. Truett, called from a lay role into ministry by a North Carolina church, and Louie D. Newton, called from a lay role as editor into ministry of the Druid Hills Baptist Church in Atlanta.[14] God may call a person directly, and he may call a person through the channel of a community. Sometimes a community is quicker to recognize an individual's gifts for ministry than the individual himself or herself.

Commonly thought of as the first deacons, the seven are described as to character and task but are not labeled deacons. They were elected by the congregation. The twelve proposed that the congregation appoint seven men of "good report" to preside over the distribution of material support to the needy among them. It is significant that this distribution was termed "the daily ministry" (Acts 6:1). The twelve wanted freedom from this ministry so that they could devote themselves fully "to prayer and the ministry of the word" (Acts 6:4). They made a sharp distinction between ministry of tables and ministry of the Word of God: "it is not proper for us to leave [literally, 'abandon'] the word of God to serve [*diakonein*—'to minister'] tables" (Acts 6:2). Such a preparation of the ministry of food and the ministry of the Word of God is a hazardous distinction, hardly to be sustained by what we read in the gospel about Jesus. It is ironic to note that those who wanted to give themselves to prayer and the Word, unencumbered by serving tables, were slower to understand and accept the gospel as including Gentiles as well as Jews. In Acts 10:1–11, 18 there were at least two of these servants of the table: Stephen, who gave his life in defending the vision (Acts 6:8–8:1), and Philip, who freely preached to Samaritans and an Ethiopian eunuch (Acts 8:4–40). Christian ministry is inspective, but there is violation when it is divided up into what may be termed secular and sacred duties. Wholeness, the concern for the total person and for all persons, belongs properly to the gospel. Jesus came to make "the whole person well," as when he healed the "lame, blind, dumb, maimed, and many others" that were cast down at his feet (Matt. 15:30–31).

Paul's call to salvation and ministry is recalled three times in Acts (9:1–19; 22:1–21; 26:1–23). Conversion and call to ministry came together in this example. Both were catastrophic and traumatic. This is understandable in view of the extreme contrast in his perspective, commitment, and value system before and after his encounter with the living Christ (Phil.

3:3–11). Some conversions and calls to ministry are like Paul's, especially for adults thus required to reverse positions that had been taken publicly and fervently. However, it is highly unlikely that many have a Damascus road experience such as the one Paul had. Background, conditioning in home or church or otherwise, and individual differences preclude any set pattern for conversion or call to ministry. God calls individuals according to his predestination.

Some people, such as Paul, know precisely when their call came, and they return often to that past experience for reassurance and direction. Others have no such traumatic experience to remember, but this does not invalidate conversion or call. Just as a person really does not remember being born into the world, the awareness of being here ("I think, therefore I am," as Rene Descartes said) suffices to assure one that there was such an experience somewhere back there. The chief evidence is in the fruit from one's ministry. This was Jesus's criterion (Matt. 7:16–20).

The call of Moses was a burning bush experience. Moses's whole experience of call to ministry was dramatic and sometimes even traumatic (Exod. 1:1–7:7). As a baby, he had to be hidden from his would-be murderers. As a youth, he was brought up in the Pharaoh's place. As a young Hebrew, he fought an Egyptian in the defense of a fellow Hebrew; he then had to flee to a distant land to avoid execution. At Horeb, he saw "the bush burned with fire, and the bush was not consumed" (Exodus 3:2), heard God's voice, and was commissioned to be the human instrument in deliverance of his people from bondage.

Not every call to ministry parallels that of Moses either in the nature of the assignment or the manner of the call. One should not doubt one's call to ministry because it does not follow the pattern experienced by Moses or others. The call comes to some quietly, without drama or trauma. For some, it comes out of a sense of human need and the sense of one's obligation to minister to that need. A sense of direction can come to any one of us, whether quietly and gently or loudly and traumatically. Differences in circumstances and differences in individuality contribute to how a call to ministry is sensed or heard. Again, not everyone must hear or experience the call in the pattern of Moses.

We generally do not think of Abraham as a minister, but he was a servant of God and played a distinctive role. Abraham was not only a servant of God through whom he laid the foundation for the people of God, first known as Israel, but he was intended from the first to reach out to all nations (Gen. 12:1–3; 17:1–4) and also to be a model in faith (Matt. 3:9; Gal. 3:15–20; Rom. 4:9–12). God called Abraham by speaking to him directly ("Go from your country and your kindred and your father's house to the land that I will show you"), promising to make of him a great nation that would be a blessing to and be blessed by "all the families of the earth" (Gen. 12:1–3).

No explanation is given as to how God was able to speak to Abraham. There is no implication that God spoke so audibly that a tape recorder could have captured the voice, and God does not speak that way to any of us, to my understanding. But in his own mysterious way, God was able to get through to Abraham and make known to him his will. Whatever may have been the influence of forces and factors in Abraham's situation is not indicated. Abraham certainly did not live in a vacuum, and it may be assumed that God spoke to him as he found him enmeshed in social activities. Beyond this simple surmise, however, it may be imprudent to say more. Our hearing may be conditioned and influenced by many factors, but hearing also implies that God in his way does speak. I remember seeing the "eyes of the Lord," but I do not believe that it was done with my natural eyes or with any particular gift that I may possess.

While yet a boy, Samuel received his call to ministry (1 Sam. 3:1–18). This call came in the quietness of the night—quietly but with increasing clarity. Samuel had every advantage of hearing God's call. His mother, Hannah, prayed for a son, and she dedicated her son to God. Samuel grew up under the care of the priest Eli, groomed for what followed. God spoke to Samuel, but it was Eli who helped him to recognize that it was the voice of God that he was hearing, not Eli's voice. This is another pattern by which some hear their call. Sometimes the influence and guidance of family or others in ministry are major factors in one's gaining a sense of direction as to ministry. This is a frequent pattern, but not all hear their call this way. Not everyone called to ministry has the help of a mother like Hannah or a priest like Eli. But one thing is for certain: the two always present are God and the one called.

We must name Ezekiel, a strange combination of prophet, priest, seer, statesman, and poet. He too came face-to-face with the Eternal, succumbed to God's glorious majesty, and accepted the destiny to which he was called. Among the hills, in the city, and in the temple, the call of the Most High came to the prophet as recorded throughout the book of Ezekiel. It effectively summoned him to God's bidding as a preacher of the ruthless word of humankind's sin and the compassionate word of humankind's deliverance. The summons came in various ways and places, but it came!

The fact of the call has significance to the prophets or preachers because of its origin in an act of God. These people did not answer the call of duty or of conscience, the call of country or of community. They responded to the call of God, the God of their fathers, the God of their nation and of its history. These facts alone may indicate their peculiar passion and their urgency of preaching the word of God. The prophet thought, believed, and preached under the influence that they had been selected and commissioned for their work by a higher power outside themselves. This power had a conscious purpose in calling them and also the ability to direct them in their activities as preachers.

Aside from the valid evidence for regarding the Bible as the authority for Christian faith and life, the fact that God did truly call his prophets, apostles, ministers, or servants (or whatever the title) to preach is fully demonstrated by the examples previously given, and by the integrity of their lives, the consistency of their teachings, and the congruity of their message with the gospel in both testaments. Without laboring over this point, we may briefly consider it. In the Bible, one can find no trace of self-delusion and fanaticism. In fact, self-delusion comes under frequent attack, as can be seen in their bitter condemnation of the false prophets or preachers or teachers.

The authenticity of the prophet's or preacher's call is assured by the close kinship of the prophetic message with the very heart of the Bible's faith and doctrine. The revelation to the prophet or the meaning of God was involved in the call itself. This revelation gave theological substance to the word that the prophet was called to preach and vitality to the contribution he made to the biblical revelation itself.

In the prophet's call, there were three elements, none of which can be disregarded. The first and greatest of these, of course, was the activity of God. The other two were closely related—the life and character of the individual prophet and the fact of his community. If God was the source and determiner of the prophet's call, the community was its object. The prophet stood between God and the community, receiving from the former what he was to give to the latter, just as the one called to preach receives revelation from God and his holy Word to use and deliver to God's people.

By steadfastly reflecting God's purpose, the one called to preach (prophet or preacher) received a regular access of new power and a continual confirmation of their original dedication to preach prophetically in his name. Their sermons were in themselves instruments of spiritual renewal. The very word of the Lord that they proclaimed was a revelatory word, not only to their people but also to the prophets and preachers themselves. This word, as it came to and was communicated by them, constantly confronted them with the meaning and wonder of God's action in the history of his people. The prophetic preacher, in this conception of his sermon, is a sinner who has learned in his own life the power of the Lord's forgiving love, his call to a new way of life, and the joy of surrender to him. The prophet testifies to what has happened to him through the grace of God. Like the apostles, they declare the wonder of what God has done for them: "They ... spoke the word of God with boldness ... With great power, the apostles gave their testimony" (Acts 4:31, 33). They make known and available to their listeners what has come to them. "But such as I have give I thee" (Acts 3:6).

In conclusion, the minister's entire professional and personal life must be viewed as a unified whole (to be discussed in the next chapter). The preachment from the pulpit and the prayer in the privacy of one's room reflect the spiritual integrity of a dedicated person, whose witness to this faith is seen in all his or her activities and words, although most clearly and forcefully in the well-prepared sermon. Prayer, Bible study, sermon preparation, and sermon delivery, as well as the preacher's integrity in community relations, fit together as expressions of a life whose passion is God alone. All that is done derives from and gives support to the preacher's devotion to the divine revealer whose Word he or she is called to preach.

True passion provides genuine motivation, deep conviction, compassionate social concern, and challenging authority for preaching the Word. It is the preachers' very lives. Without it, they communicate no commanding truth to lift humans up to God or to reveal them to themselves. This passion indicates both why they must preach and what they must preach. It marks their call to preach as well as the reason for their coming, for God has commissioned them to preach a special word to humankind. This word is sure to be preached with power (also discussed in the next part) when the one called deeply experiences the presence of the one who is the source.

PART 2

PROPHECY AND PREACHING

THE BACKGROUND OF PROPHECY

Today, the term *prophecy* suggests a variety of meanings. We speak of prophets of the weather, prophets of the news, and prophets who champion a social call. Even when there is some interest in biblical prophecy, understanding is distorted by those who sometimes give the impression that the biblical prophet gazed into God's crystal ball and predicted the shape of things to come. It is evident that many are ignorant or the role of the Old Testament prophets and fail to understand properly the spiritual legacy that we have received from them.

What is a prophet? Our English word comes to us from the Greek word *prophetes*, which literally means "one who speaks for another, especially for the gods." This Greek word, in turn, is a fairly accurate way to render the Hebrew word *nabi*, which refers to "one who communicates the divine will."[1] We can get an idea of how the prophet's role was understood in ancient Israel by looking at a couple of passages that deal with the relationship between Moses and Aaron (Exod. 4:14–16; 7:1–2). Here, the language is used figuratively. Moses was to be, as it were, "God" to Aaron, and Aaron was to be Moses's nabi. That is, Moses was to tell Aaron what to say, and Aaron was to speak on behalf of Moses to Pharaoh. On the basis of this analogy, it is clear that the prophet was regarded as a person through whom God speaks to people. Called to be God's spokesman, they received the promise that God's words would be put in their mouths (Jer. 1:9).

Studies of the forms of prophetic speech have shown that the prophets often employed a messenger style, which was well-known in the ancient world.[2] For example, when Jacob was returning to his homeland, he bridged the distance between himself and his brother Esau by sending messengers: "And Jacob sent messengers before him … instructing them, 'Thus you shall say to my lord Esau: "Thus says your servant Jacob, 'I have sojourned …'"'" (Gen. 32:3, 4). Note that almost the same language is used in prophetic oracles. The prophets understood themselves to be sent. They have received God's commission: "Go and say to my people." A prophetic message often begins with the formula "Thus saith the Lord" and concludes with "the oracle of God" or "saith the Lord" (Amos 1:3–5; Jer. 2:1–3; Isa. 45:11–13). All this indicates that the prophets thought of themselves as messengers sent to communicate "the word of the Lord" to the people. Their authority lay not in themselves—in their religious experience or in their opinions—but in the one who had sent them: "Thus says the Lord."

The purpose of God's speaking through his prophet was not to communicate information about events in the distant future. But these predictions, some of which came true and some of which did not, had reference to the immediate future and depended on the present and on the response of the hearers. To be sure, the prophets often made predictions in the conviction that God was shaping the course of events according to his purpose. When a doctor makes a prediction that a patient has only a short time to live, it makes the patient's present moments more precious and serious. And so the prophet's announcement of what God was about to do accented the urgency of the present. The prophet was to communicate God's message for now and to summon the people to respond today.[3]

THE PROPHET

The prophet is a person who acts as the organ of divine communication with men, especially with regard to revealed things. The prophet differs from the priest in representing the divine side of the mediation, while the priest rather acts from the human side. The term *prophet* is an anglicized Greek word and denotes one who speaks for another or in another's name. The Hebrew term rendered *prophet* is thought by some to signify one elevated or excited, so as to pour forth animated oracles or, according to others, a person imbued with the Spirit of God. Strictly speaking, a prophet is one to whom the knowledge of secret things is revealed, whether past (John 4:19—"The woman saith unto him, Sir, I perceive that thou art a prophet. This knowledge about her past life startled her and she concluded that He was a prophet with power, and she quickly changed the subject lest He expose more of her life"), present (2 Kings 5:26—"And he said unto him, went not mine heart with thee, when the man turned again from his chariot to meet thee? Is it a time to receive money, and to receive garments, and olive yards, and vineyards, and sheep, and oxen, and menservants, and maidservants?—the prophet saw his doings as he carried them out."), or to come (Luke 1:76–79—"And thou, child, shall be called the prophet of the Highest: for thou shalt go before the face of the Lord to prepare his ways; to give knowledge of salvation unto his people by the remission of their sins, through the tender mercy of our God; whereby the dayspring from on high hath visited us, to give light to them that sit in darkness and in the shadow of death, to guide our feet into the way of peace." In remission of sins, all have a personal knowledge of salvation.).

Different modes appear to have been employed to convey to the prophets the knowledge of future events. Events seem to have passed before their minds, like a picture or panorama whereby the objects and symbols were presented to the prophetic eye. Even waking and sleeping episodes, and perhaps a still small voice, but in whatever form the communication was made, the impression was undoubtedly as distinct and vivid as were those objects of an ocular vision. The prophets did not always know the meaning of what was communicated to them; hence, Daniel and John found it necessary to make inquiries as to the meaning of certain portions of the revelations, and they were distinctly explained to them: "And it came to pass, when I, even I Daniel, had seen the vision, and *sought for the meaning*, then, behold, there stood before me as the appearance of a man" (Dan. 8:15ff). Daniel sought for the true meaning of his vision so as to pass on to us a picture of world events at the end of time. Revelation 17:6ff says, "And I saw the woman drunken with the blood of the saints, and with the blood of the martyrs of Jesus; and when I saw her, I wondered with great admiration. And the angel said unto me, wherefore didst thou marvel? I will tell thee the mystery of the woman, and of the beast that carrieth her, which hath the seven heads and ten horns." John was given the answer to the vision because of prayerful speculation.

The term *prophecy* is the foretelling of events through divine revelation. If it is not true prophecy, it will usually be perceived (Neh. 6:12). Prophecy is sometimes used analogically—"Follow after charity, and desire spiritual gifts, but rather that ye may prophesy ... he that prophesieth speaketh unto men to edification, and exhortation, and comfort ... he that prophesieth edifieth the church" (1 Cor. 14:1ff)—probably because those who exercised these functions were regarded as under the direction of the Holy Spirit. So it is said that Judas and Silas were prophets and that in Acts 13:1, there were in the church at Antioch certain prophets and teachers—that is, official instructors (1 Cor. 12:28; Eph. 2:20; Rev. 18:20). In the Old Testament, the term *prophet* is also applied to the sacred musicians (1 Chron. 25:1ff—"Moreover David and the captains of the host separated to the service of the sons of Asaph, and of Heman, and of Jeduthun, who should prophesy with harps, with psalteries, and with cymbals"), and it may be only because Miriam led the concert (Exod. 15:20–21) that she was reckoned as a prophetess. Aaron is spoken of as a prophet (Exod. 7:1), being one who delivered another's message. Abraham is also called a prophet (Gen. 20:7), one who bore a near and peculiar relation to God. Isaiah, Jeremiah, Ezekiel, and Daniel are called the greater prophets because of the size of their books and the extent and importance of their prophecies. Joel, Jonah, Amos, Hosea, Micah, Nahum, Zephaniah, Habakkuk, Obadiah, Haggai, Zechariah, and Malachi are called the minor or lesser prophets[4] for the same reasons.

THE PROPHET OFFICE

The first person whom the Bible calls a prophet (from the Hebrew word *abhi*) was Abraham (Gen. 20:7), but Old Testament prophecy received its normative form in the life and person of Moses, who constituted a standard of comparison for all future prophets (Deut. 18:15–19; 34:10). As mentioned, he received a special and personal call from God. The initiative in making a prophet rests with God (Exod. 3:1–4; 17), and it is only the false prophet who dares to take the office upon himself (Jer. 14:14; 23:21). The primary object and effect of the call was an introduction into God's presence. This was the "secret" or "counsel" of the Lord (1 Kings 22:19; Jer. 23:22; Amos 3:7). The prophet stood before others as a man who had been made to stand before God (1 Kings 17:1; 18:15). Moses was not left to struggle for the meaning or events as or after they happened; he was forewarned of events and of their significance by the verbal communications of God. So it was with all the prophets.

Many of the prophets were found confronting their kings and playing an active, statesman's part in national affairs. This was a function of the prophet that found its prototype in Moses, who legislated for the nation and was even called king (Deut. 33:5). We also see in Moses that combination of proclamation and prediction that is found in all the prophets. It is this interlocking of proclamation and prediction that distinguishes the true prophet from the mere prognosticator.[5] Many of the prophets used symbols in the delivery of their message (Jer. 19:1ff; Ezek. 4:11ff.). Moses used the uplifted hand (Exod. 17:8ff.) and the uplifted serpent (Num. 21:8). And finally, the intercessory aspect of the prophetic task was also displayed in him. He was "for the people to Godward" (Exod. 18:19; Num. 27:5), and on at least one notable occasion, he literally stood in the breach as a man of prayer (Exod. 32:30ff; Deut. 9:18ff.).

The Prophet's Purpose

Obviously, the prophet was first a man of God. It was the prophet's conviction that the proclamation of God's Word radically changed the whole situation. The Word is an active ingredient added to the situation, which is henceforth impelled forward in terms of the word spoken (Isa. 40:8; 55:11). Clearly the prophets spoke about their situation primarily by means of warnings and encouragements concerning the future. If people were to exercise due moral responsibility in the present, they should be aware of the future. Calls to repentance and calls to holiness were equally based on a word concerning the future; the vision of wrath to come was made the basic of a present seeking of the mercy of God, and the vision of bliss to come calls to a walking in the light.

The prophet's whole prophetic career had a clear purpose even as each speech was associated with a definitive objective. Thus, we are concerned here with both the immediate aims and the ultimate goals of the prophet as preacher. Whether the two kinds of purposes are related remains to be seen. I believe that they should be. But the one called to preach should be aware of pressures that are exerted upon the modern minister to deviate from the path of faithfulness to their call. This may suggest why their professed purpose to be called of God may not always motivate them in preaching. This could also have been the case with the prophets of Israel. In all probability, complete consistency was not any easier for them than it is now.

The true prophet, however, finds time to stand in the council of the Lord. When they do this, they hear God's Word of salvation for his people and also for themselves as they fight to keep their calling from being defied. This is the only way they can hold fast to their true purpose in life. What is the true purpose of the faithful prophet? The main aim of the prophet is to be God's spokesman. They are to be unequivocally devoted to the utterance of the divine word to the people of the community of faith. This word must be spoken, lest they be untrue to their call to preach and their people perish in their persistent rebellion.

More specifically, the prophet must serve as a watchman over God's flock. Prophets must be on the lookout for evidence of wickedness, disobedience, and disloyalty to the Lord. These evils, if undetected and unchecked, would destroy God's community, to which he had chosen to demonstrate his love. This evaluation would be derived from an extraordinary sensitivity of the prophet's spirit and mind. It would demand of the prophet a unique realization of the work of God in history as transmitted through tradition and made known more directly through personal communion and worship. Just what this means for modern prophets when they fulfill the role of a prophetic watchman today is very clear. True prophets can carry out their mission and fulfill their purpose by looking at history with the eyes of faith. Faith can be renewed and empowered by contact with the living Christ, even while he watches from within his study.

We have seen that the great purpose of the prophet is to

function as a man of God, his spokesman, dedicated completely to the work of making known the word of salvation to his people. This word that they must communicate is a word of judgment and redemption, a word of righteousness and compassion. It is also a sacramental word whereby the very presence of the Savior God may be realized. The prophet is a speaker, a teacher, and a representative of the Lord God, who in the fullness of time appeared in Jesus Christ. With this background of an understanding of the great purpose and task of the one called to preach, we may now investigate the objectives of preaching, which are varied and many. We will also want to look at the things that pertain to preaching, such as the preacher, the sermon, the construction of the sermon, and all the aspects of delivering the message. Some discussing will be made on other authors' views on preaching and homiletics in general.

Modes of Communication

The prophets came before their contemporaries as men with a word to say. The spoken oracle is the form in which the Word of God is expressed. Each prophet or person called to preach stamps the marks of his own personality and experience on this word. For example, the oracles of Jeremiah and Ezekiel are as distinct as the personalities of the two prophets.

Sometimes the prophets couched their oracles in the form of parable or allegory (e.g., Isa. 5:1–7; 2 Sam. 12:1–7; and especially Ezek. 16 and 23), but the most dramatic presentation of their message was by means of the "acted oracle." It was a visual aid, but in association with the Hebrew notion of the efficacy of the Word, it served to make the discharge of the Word into the contemporary situation more powerful. This is best seen in the dialogue between the dying Elisha and the king Joash

(2 Kings 13:14–19). In verse 17, the arrow of the Lord's victory is shot against Syria, and thereby the prophet introduced the king into a sphere of symbolic action. The Word embodied in the symbol is exceedingly effective; it cannot fail to come to pass, and it will accomplish exactly what the symbol declared. Other examples of symbolic action are when Isaiah woke up naked and barefoot (Isa. 20), Jeremiah smashed a potter's vessel in the place of potsherds (Jer. 19), Ahijah tore his new coat in twelve pieces and gave Jeroboam ten (1 Kings 11:29ff.), and Ezekiel besieged a model city (Ezek. 4:1–3), dug through the house wall (Ezek. 12:1ff.), and did not mourn for his dead wife (Ezek. 24:15ff.). Thus, the acted oracle was a movement of God to humankind. It was an activity on which God had already decided. The initiative rested solely with God.

Parables and other figures of speech are common. The prophets drew their language and imagery from the routine experiences of their people. They had no opportunity in their culture to learn elaborate creedal statements on which they might expatiate profoundly in the presence of their congregation after completing their studies and embarking upon their ministry. The parables of the vineyard, the pottery, the wine jars, the broken flask, the figs, the valley of dry bones, and the two sticks drew largely upon popular experience, as did the great number of references to familiar objects—the harlot, a wounded man, an ox, an ass, the bee (for Assyria), a mighty stream, shimmering summer heat, and the storm.[6] There are also allusions to birds, plant life, sun, moon, eclipse, earthquake, clouds, mountains, and desert. There are similes, metaphors, personification, hyperbole, and every other literary device that would promote vivid and effective speech. The concrete and picturesque style of the prophetic preacher derives from the nature both of the Hebrew language, which was their vehicle, and from the message, which they were required to communicate. They were not called to make clear, abstract truths about theology or the moral problems. Rather, they were moved to be a prophet to announce God's action in history and the need for humankind's response.

Training

Many of the early prophets belonged to guilds or schools, which were known as "the sons of the prophets." They lived in communities, where they were under the leadership of a chief prophet who was apparently known as their father. Elijah and Elisha, for instance, were leaders of prophetic communities at Bethel, Jericho, and Gilgal (2 Kings 2:3–4; 4:38). These guilds were not tied permanently to any one place but were free to travel around and deliver oracles as the occasion demanded.[7] There also existed among the Hebrews, as part of their system of priesthood, a regular order of prophets, and a fixed institution in which prophets were educated. This institution was created by Samuel, who was highly praised for his work (Jer. 15:1; Acts 3:24). Schools were founded at Ramah (1 Sam. 19:19), Bethel (2 Kings 2:3), Jericho (2 Kings 2:5), Gilgal (2 Kings 4:38), and more. Young men were instructed there in the interpretation of the law, in music, and in poetry by some older prophet who was called father and master, as previously noted. However, there was no connection between the prophetical education and the prophetical gifts.[8] Doubtless many young men went through the prophetical school without ever receiving a message from God. Though Amos had not attended any school, he was called by God. Amos 7:14 says expressly that he was "no prophet nor a prophet's son"—that is, not trained in the schools as one of the so-called sons of the prophets—but that he was a shepherd and gardener.[9] But this disclaimer seems to refer to his occupation prior to his call and to lack of technical preparation for his work, rather than authorization: "and the Lord said unto me, Go, prophesy unto my people Israel" (7:15).

PREACHING

What Is Preaching?

In the New Testament, preaching is "the public proclamation of Christianity to the non-Christian world."[†] It is not religious discourse to a closed group of initiates but an open and public proclamation of God's redemptive activity in and through Jesus Christ. Dr. C. H. Dodd has pointed out that the New Testament writers draw a clear distinction between preaching (kerygma) and teaching (didache). Teaching is, in a large majority of cases, ethical instruction. Preaching, on the other hand, is the public proclamation to the non-Christian world. For the early church, then, to preach the gospel was by no means the same thing as to deliver moral exhortation. It was by kerygma, says Paul, not by didache, that it pleased God to save humankind. Preaching is not primarily instruction. A sermon may contain argument. We may (and should) build up systematic arguments to convince the minds of our hearers. The sermon may also include moral instruction or exhortation arising from the truth that has been proclaimed. It may offer a great deal that is profitable in all kinds of ways, but it if does not contain proclamation, it is not preaching. And it must be the proclamation of the gospel, the

---

[†] C. H. Dodd, *The Apostolic Preaching and Its Development,* 7.

good news (Luke 4:18, 43; Rom. 1:15; 1 Cor. 1:17; Eph. 1:3), or what God has done, is doing, and will do.

The choice of verbs in the Greek New Testament for the activity of preaching points us back to its original meaning. The most characteristic is *kerysso*, "to proclaim as a herald." In the ancient world, the herald was a figure of considerable importance. Preaching is heralding; the message proclaimed is the glad tidings of salvation. Whereas *kerysso* tells us something about the activity of preaching, *evangelizomai*, "to bring good news," emphasizes the quality of the message itself.

True preaching is best understood in terms of its relation to the wider theme of revelation. Revelation is essentially God's self-disclosure apprehended by the response of faith. Because Calvary is God's supreme self-revelation, the problem is how God can reveal himself in the present through an act and humankind's apprehension of it. It is the medium through which God contemporizes his historic self-disclosure in Christ and offers humankind the opportunity to respond in faith (Rom. 10:17).

This proclamation (preaching) is threefold:

1. We are to proclaim the historical facts through which God revealed himself and acted for humankind's salvation. These facts are the birth, life, cross, and resurrection of Jesus (1 Cor. 1:18, 23; Acts 17:18). "God was in Christ, reconciling the world unto himself" (2 Cor.5:19). The gospel that Paul believed himself called to preach was not a story that he had invented. It was a gospel that had been entrusted to him by God. "But as we were allowed of God to be put in trust with the Gospel, even so we speak" (1 Thess. 2:4). The gospel he received had been handed on to him in the Christian tradition by those who themselves had firsthand knowledge of the facts. "For I delivered unto you first of all that which

I received, how that Christ died for our sins according to the Scriptures; And that he was buried, and that he rose again the third day according to the Scriptures" (1 Cor. 15:2f.). Hence, our gospel is "the faith once delivered to the saints" (Jude 1:3), delivered to Paul, delivered to every true preacher since, and it is ours to proclaim.

2. We are to proclaim what God has done through Christ in human experience. "By the grace of God I am what I am" (1 Cor. 15:10). Preachers must proclaim the grace of God from their own experience and observation. They have seen what God can do in the twentieth century as well as in the first. Above all, preachers must speak with a conviction born of the knowledge that God has been at work in their own soul.

3. We must claim that what God has done for others and for ourselves He can do, and will do, for any person. There is no good news in the affirmation that God's saving power was given to humans centuries ago, or to me yesterday, unless I can assure the neediest hearer that it will be given to them today. There is no gospel in condemnation or in confronting people with moral demands to which they know that they will never be able to respond in their own strength. The gospel is the good news of God's promises made freely and unconditionally to any person who will receive them in simple trust—promises that are utterly reliable. "No one who puts his trust in Him will ever be disappointed. No one."[10]

It is clear, then, that when one preaches, they are not merely making a speech or giving an address. The preacher preaches on behalf of God as though God was entreating by them. We can go further. Preaching is not the activity of humankind alone; it is not merely a person who is speaking. God is speaking through the person. In other words, when preaching, the preacher is an inspired person, if the unction of the Spirit is upon him or her. However, this is not always the case. But the word *inspiration* is used with such a wide range of meaning that I will shed more light on the meaning as used here under "The Preacher's Authority" in part 3.

The Purpose of Preaching

What, then, is the purpose of preaching? The purpose of preaching is to make articulate the whole message that comes through a person's relationship to God and to his people. The glory of preaching is to tell humankind that they do have a friend and to make their hearts as well as their minds believe. It is a friend who is stronger than wickedness and stronger than worldliness, and who by his immortality can set them free from every degrading force that holds them down. Preaching proclaims the message of what the apostle Paul called "Christ in you, the hope of glory" (Col. 1:27). Preaching explains the meaning of the redeemed life, which is the shared inheritance of the Christian fellowship. Preaching seeks to interest, convince, persuade, and move. Therefore, preaching is the effective communication of divine truth in the Christian scriptures, by one called of God to witness for him of a redemptive deed for the purpose of giving eternal life through Jesus Christ.

The Importance of Preaching

The importance of preaching is for the guidance and help of human souls. It is important because it is a communication from the living God to living souls. Preaching can make life different for everyone who hears it. The total objective is to bring life to the people. Through preaching, six basic needs of the congregation are met: (1) people are saved, (2) they grow in devotion to God, (3) they develop more mature understanding of God's truth, (4) they live in better relationship with others, (5) they serve God in a more dedicated way, and (6) they find strength and comfort in trouble. It is the proclamation of a decisive event. The power and love of God in Christ have broken the control over people of the evil to which they were in bondage. That power and love, alive and operative, brings the eternal promise: "I am come that they may have life, and that they may have it more abundantly" (John 10:10). Preaching is important because the messenger has a message of authority from another—God.

THE PREACHING EVENT

Once called to preach, the novice preacher will want to read books on preaching for further understanding on their calling to preach. One such book is *The Preaching Event: The Lyman Beecher Lectures* by John S. Claypool.[11] This small volume consists of five chapters: "The Preaching Event," "The Preacher as Reconciler," "The Preacher as Gift-Giver," "The Preacher as Witness," and "The Preacher as Nurturer." Chapters 2–5 describe the what, why, how, and when of the preaching event, respectively.

The author thoroughly bares his soul on the subject of confessional preaching. He believes an approach is a valid one after a decade of preaching. Notwithstanding the controversy that our stories can get in the way of the great story and deflect attention to the wrong place, Claypool says that if motives are genuine and not acquisitive, and when one's purpose is to make healing contact with the depths of another, these experiences (drawn from the reservoir of one's own living) can be a powerful resource. Claypool outlines the values and perils of making personal experiences a pastoral resource for the preaching event. He states, "What happens to us can creatively happen through us," and he notes that many parts of the great story would never have been known had personal experiences not been shared with others. For example, Mary's conception by the Holy Spirit and Jesus's experience of the temptations in the wilderness both took place in utter privacy. St. Paul was by no means hesitant to tell of his life-changing encounter on the Damascus Road. Neither was Peter reluctant to share how he had denied the Lord when no other of the twelve, only Jesus, was present to witness the event. These things bring strength to his convictions.

In "The Preacher as Reconciler," Claypool states the preacher must work to establish a relation of trust at the deepest level between human creatures and the Creator. This is the true objective of the preacher as reconciler. The story the Christian preacher has to tell is the story of a God whose only reason for creating was his desire to share the wonder of his aliveness and who, in the face of utterly erroneous suspicion, has refused to stop loving or to give up on creation but moves to repair the damage and affirm that he really is for us and not against us.

In "The Preacher as Gift-Giver," Claypool affirms that the sense of grace should be the foundation of all things. The preacher takes what has blessed them and offers it in hopes of blessings others. The preacher is then the "gift-giver." The preacher transfers the value of God's love to the congregation and does not need confirmation from others to have a sense of worth about the message preached. Preachers' sense of worth come from their needs having been met healthily. The preaching event should be aimed primarily at giving, rather than getting. Claypool describes it as a kind of transaction that can only become what it is meant to be when preachers come to see themselves as gifts and turn to be gift-givers to others. Preaching as a form of gift-love then is possible. The central affirmation of the Bible is that God's love is gift-love and not need-love. The preachers make available to the congregation that which has enriched themselves, namely, God's love.

In "The Preacher as Witness," Claypool acknowledges that instead of trying to dazzle people with the breadth of learning or to pass on lots of secondhand information that may or may not be existentially relevant to their situations, we can help most when we are honest enough to lay bare our own wounds and acknowledge what is saving and helping us. When what is being shared has authenticated itself in the crucible of one's own experience and is of vital necessity to the other, Claypool asserts this makes for a powerful transaction indeed.

In "The Preacher as Nurturer," Claypool examines the issue of timeliness. He examines what role the reality of time plays in the act of preaching. There are teachable moments and appropriate occasions when things are possible that could never have been before and never could be again. This is a factor, Claypool states, which Christian preachers must take into account if they want to speak home to the hearts of their hearers in a way that can effectively help reestablish a relation of trust between them and the Creator. He examines what the preacher as nurturer must do. First, he suggests that preachers acquaint themselves with the general contour of the human saga, from infancy to old age. Second, preachers must learn how to listen carefully and perceptively. He cites Paul Tillich's famous method of correlation, in which he suggests that we let culture define the questions and revelation provide the answers as a fine working model for authentic preaching.

Finally, he asserts that what we are trying to do in the preaching event—the preacher as a reconciler, gift-giver, witness, and nurturer—is to participate in the restoring of a relation of trust between human creatures and the Creator. Why do this? It's not to get something for ourselves in gift-love. Rather, how should we do it? By making available as witnesses what we have learned from our own wounded-ness for the benefit of the wounded-ness of others. When do we do this? At times and in ways that are appropriate to another's growing, as a farmer nurtures a crop. To do this is to participate in the extension of the gospel into our own time.

In examining the various roles of the preacher, Claypool demonstrates that preaching undertaken faithfully and in recognition of its full potential is one of the most powerful ways a preacher can affect the lives of other people. It is an awesome task to perform. Preachers must do far more than move people in a level of behavior and must establish trust at the deepest level, to participate in a level of primal reconciliation. I strongly recommend the reading of this book for growth and a deeper spiritual insight.

Another book of interest to those called to preach is *How Shall They Preach: The Lyman Beecher Lectures* by Dr. Gardner C. Taylor.[12] This small but powerful volume consists of two parts. Part 1 is "The Lyman Beecher Lectureship on Preaching, Yale Divinity School, 1975–76," consisting of four lectures. Part 2 is "Five Lenten Sermons" by one of the nation's most respected African American preachers.

In his prologue to *How Shall They Preach*, the author cites a paradox in reflecting on the preaching enterprise after forty years of practicing the craft, and the impossibility of setting forth the foolishness of preaching, which constitutes at the same time a part of the wisdom of God. He cites the apostle Paul's examination of the grand pyramid of salvation in Jesus Christ as its apex, as revealed in his letter to the Romans: "For whosoever shall call upon the name of the Lord shall be saved" (Rom. 10:13). The writer concludes that this is what it is all about: the end and purpose of the whole biblical revelation, culminating in the incredible Christ event. With some reflection, the writer states that the work of the preacher is fundamental to this process.

Several questions are addressed as the author attempts to examine the preaching enterprise: How shall they preach except they be sent? How are they who preach to look upon their work? What shall arm preachers, particularly in a skeptical time like our own, with the boldness required of the herald of God? What shall disarm preachers from thinking too highly of themselves than they ought? Dr. Taylor expressed concern that we may exult in our calling when we hear the apostle's words, "How shall they hear without a preacher?" How shall we utter, and by what power, so that it will rise up out of our minds and hearts, fall on ears of individuals, and please God in so doing? In hope, the message is carried to the depths of the hearers' hearts, to be seen again in their lives, and the witness that they make to their communities.

In lecture 1, "Recognizing and Removing the Presumptuousness of Preaching," the author argues (sometimes with what appears to be deliberate contradictions) that "measured by almost any gauge, preaching is a presumptuous business." Dr. Taylor asserts that if the preaching enterprise does not have some sanctions beyond ordinary human reckoning, then it is indeed rash and audacious for one person to dare to stand up before or among other people and declare that he or she brings from the eternal God a message for those who listen that involves issues of nothing less than those of life and death. Dr. Taylor believes that the role of the preacher would be more reasonable to the mind if they who preach could assert truthfully that they enjoy, by virtue of their office as preacher, a moral superiority to those to whom they address the gospel.

Other topics covered in the lecture series are "The Foolishness of Preaching," "Building a Sermon," and "Preaching the Whole Counsel of God." I strongly recommend reading the entire lecture series for all who are called to preach without regard to race, gender, age, or personal circumstances. Each lecture presents powerful arguments and the seasoned wisdom of one who has preached and practiced preaching with a special anointing for more than forty years.

HOMILETICS LECTURES

A neophyte preacher should find books on homiletics interesting. *The Preacher's Manual: A Study in Homiletics* by Dr. John H. C. Fritz is a good one to start with.[13] This powerful volume consists of three parts: "A Study in Homiletics with a Brief History of Preaching," "Sermon Studies and Sermons Outlines," "Texts for Various Occasions and the Periscopic Systems," by contemporary preachers such as John A. Broadus, Austin Phelps, Christian Palmer, M. Reu, and T. Hardwood Pattison. I will limit the discussion to part 1, "A Study in Homiletics."

In the prologue to *The Preacher's Manual*, the author states that he encourages good preaching by making the fundamentals in homiletics stand out, and by presenting what has been the crux of homileticians—the sermon method—in such a way as not to exhaust or bewilder the beginner and, at the same time, keep the busy pastor in mind who desires quickly "to brush up" on the essential things that make for good preaching. He states that the scriptures themselves are often overlooked when speaking of books that give directions for good sermonizing. The scriptures speak not only of the contents of the Christian sermon, but also of the manner of presentation. For example: "Preach the word" (2 Tim. 4:2); "I determined not to know anything among you save Jesus Christ, and him crucified" (1

Cor. 2:2); "We preach not ourselves but Christ Jesus, the Lord" (2 Cor. 4:5); "In the Church I had rather speak five words with my understanding, that by my voice I might teach others also, than ten thousand words in an unknown tongue" (1 Cor. 14:19); "And Ezra, the scribe, stood upon a pulpit of wood, which they had made for the purpose ... And Ezra opened the Book in the sight of all the people (for he was above the people); and when he opened it, all the people stood up ... So they read in the Book of the Law of God distinctly and gave the *sense and caused them to understand the reading*" (Neh. 8:4–8; emphasis added); "And the Levites shall speak and say unto all the men of Israel *with a loud voice*" (Deut. 27:14; emphasis added); and "My speech and my preaching was not *with enticing words of man's wisdom* but in demonstration of the Spirit and of power" (1 Cor. 2:4; emphasis added). Also, from the addresses delivered by the prophets and apostles, we can learn how the Word should be preached, especially from the discourses of Jesus, the model preacher of all times.

On preaching, the author discusses at length the authority to preach, what to preach, the purpose of preaching, the importance of preaching well, and learning to preach. He cites that the technique of the sermon does not essentially differ from that of any ordinary literary composition, speech, or address, but the sermon differs essentially in the source of its material, which should always be the Word of God, and in its purpose, which should always be the salvation of blood-bought souls and the glory of God. He says that homiletics supplies the rules for the making of the sermon, which are best learned by the inductive method. He says that praying for divine blessing is essential. When preachers read their Bibles and study their sermon texts, they should pray for divine enlightenment. Not mere erudition, and not even much theological learning, will suffice to open for us the meaning of scripture: that alone the Spirit of God can do, for the things of the Spirit of God must be spiritually discerned.

Dr. Fritz states that there are three homiletic requisites: a thorough study and understanding of the text, a good outline, and a good delivery. He calls this the process of sermonizing. He then gives an outline for each with an explanation. He discusses the chief rules for choosing a text, and the meaning and purposes of the periscopes along with its history. After all this, he treats the two sermon methods that he says refers to the treatment of the text. The methods are the direct or analytical method and the indirect or synthetic method. Next, he examines the various sermon methods of some homileticians. The methods are topical, textual, expository, and inferential. In evaluating these methods, Dr. Fritz states that (1) if a preacher uses a text at all, he should preach that text, and (2) there are only two ways in which any text can be treated, by saying either what the text says in so many words or what is implied in the text.

Continuing with part 1, Dr. Fritz asserts that unless preachers present the specific thought of their text, they are not preaching that text. The theme of the sermon should present the subject matter of the text in a brief, concise, easily understood form. It may be in the form of a declarative sentence, a question, or a mere assertion. He discusses the treatment of the text in a specific way as opposed to its treatment in a general way, and how sermonizers must therefore find the dividing point of their theme, which may be a word or a phrase. A theme is usually divided into two or three chief or main parts, seldom more, states Fritz. He thoroughly discusses the application of the text, the introduction, which should be thought of last but written first and should gain the interest of the hearer for the theme, and the conclusion, which should make sure that the hearer has gotten the theme (or in other words, the text). In the conclusion, the sermon should reach its climax. He explains in a general way that the conclusion should not be a repetition but a brief summary.

Dr. Fritz also tells why illustrations should be used. The most effective way of presenting a true conception of a concrete object is to present the object itself. But if this cannot be done, Fritz says, a picture of the object will give a better understanding of the object in a few minutes than a long description of it. It's a picture we present to the hearer by means of illustration. Our word picture brings to the mind of the hearer an object that he or she sees. Fritz discusses how to use the simile and the metaphor as illustration, and also how to use anecdote and the short story to illustrate. The best sources of illustrations are the Bible and everyday life with which the hearers are familiar.

Other topics covered in part 1 are the language of the sermon, making the sermon interesting, the length of the sermon, writing and memorizing the sermon, the revision of the manuscript, the pulpit greeting, the address to the hearers, reading the text, the delivery of the sermon, the printed sermon, hindering the work of the Holy Spirit, fundamental homiletics rules, the various use of scriptures in the sermon, law and gospel in the sermon, the parable texts, the miracle texts, occasional sermons and addresses, the Old Testament as sermon material, the periscopic systems, and the history of preaching. This is an exciting manual for both the novice preacher and the experienced preacher. It will provide constant companionship to its reader for years; its very nature suggests it. I strongly recommend the reading of the entire manual for all who desire to prepare and deliver effective sermons.[2]

In time, those called to preach will want to read books by

some great theologians. One of the most influential theologians of the twentieth century was Karl Barth, a professor of systematic theology at the University of Basel, Switzerland.[14] In Barth's book *Homiletics,* he links theology and preaching. He believed that theology should be nothing other than sermon preparation. Following his lectures closely will allow the reader to enter his theological world. Preachers will find that the central trust of his work is a call to fidelity of the gospel. The work of conversion or decision is not placed upon the shoulders of the preacher, but that of grace alone through the working of the Holy Spirit. The preacher, justified by God's free grace, speaks as a forgiven sinner to forgiven sinners and is blessed (sanctified) by the gospel.

Barth banishes introductions from sermons, which is a peculiar position. Equally peculiar is the fact that he condemns the whole idea of conclusion to sermons, fearing that an ending will either be a "work" or a weakening of the message of application. In *Homiletics,* Barth suggests that preachers risk no more than a reiteration of the text. He is uncompromisingly biblical and fears an admixture of the scripture's message with the preacher's own cultural thoughts. Barth calls ministers to "active expectation" and "ongoing submission" in their study of the Bible. Although much is beyond the scope of this book, we will observe Barth's thoughts and theology as they relate to sermon preparation, which after all is nothing other than theology, according to Barth.

In chapter 1, part 1, "The Nature of the Sermon," Barth gives a historical and dogmatic sketch of the definitions and criticism of what preaching is by such men as David Hollaz, Friedrich Schleiermacher, Alexander Vinet, Christian Palmer, C. I. Nitzsch, Johannes Bauer, Karl Fezer, and Leonhard Fendt. Barth states with explanations that a definition of preaching will have nine constitutive elements: (1) revelation of the Word of God, (2) the church as the place of preaching, (3) the divine command, (4) the special ministry of the preacher, (5) the thought of preaching as an attempt, (6) the relation to scripture, (7) the concept of individual speech, (8) the concept of the congregation, and (9) the Holy Spirit as the starting point, center, and conclusion.

In chapter 1, part 2, "An Attempt at a New Definition," Barth states two definitions: (1) "Preaching is the Word of God which he himself speaks, claiming for the purpose the exposition of a biblical text in free human words that are relevant to contemporaries by those who are called to do this in the church that is obedient to its commission" and (2) Preaching is the attempt enjoined upon the church to serve God's own Word, through one who is called thereto, by expounding a biblical text in human words and making it relevant to contemporaries in intimation of what they have to hear from God Himself." He says, "Externally these two formulas contain all that we have come up with thus far. The same elements occur in both, each in its own place, each seen from the decisive standpoint. Together they form the answer to the question of the relation between the Word of God and the human word. The totality forms a closed circle that begins with God and ends with him" (p. 44).

Behind these two definitions stands the decisive statement of Christology regarding the unity between God and us in Jesus Christ. The difficulty of preaching, according to Barth, is none other than trying to say who and what Jesus Christ is. Preaching must go both ways: the way of descending thought and the way of ascending thought. As pointing fingers or signposts, they can only brokenly and very imperfectly discharge their mission as proclaimers of God's Word. Two things call for emphasis: First, God is the one who works, and second, we humans can try to point to what is said in scripture. There is no third thing, Barth says. The concept of preaching cannot be fixed on the basis of experiences. It is a theological concept that arises in the faith that can only point to the divine reality.

In chapter 2, "Criteria of the Sermon," Barth explains the nine elements.

1. Revelation. Barth says that preaching must conform to revelation and that preaching cannot try to be a proof of the truth of God. Preaching may not try to create the reality of God. Therefore, the task is to build up the kingdom of God, convert, or lead to decision. It must bring to light our situation and set us before God. Barth's thoughts are that our preaching today differs from the prophets and apostles who saw and touched Christ, not qualitatively, but it differs in as much as it is done in a different place. Barth explains that preaching must be exposition of holy scriptures. Our task, he says, is simply to follow the distinctive movement of thought in the text and not with a plan that arises out of it. He cautions against becoming a pope of the congregation (presenting own ideas instead of God's Word). The central point of all preaching is solely what God has done with us in Christ (Immanuel, "God with us"), states Barth.

Another criterion of the sermon is that it must have thrust. Barth believes that the sermon takes on thrust when it comes from Christ and not so much as getting the attention of the listeners. He explains that one automatically gets to the people when proceeding from Christ due to the fact that: "The Word was made flesh" and "can be spoken legitimately only when there follows at once: Amen, come, Lord Jesus" (p. 54).

Preachers should simply believe the gospel and say all they have to say on the basis of this belief. This means that the thrust of the sermon is always downhill, not uphill to a goal. Everything has already taken place. Preaching, Barth explains, stands between the First Advent and the Second Advent, and so does the whole life of the Christian. Christian preaching, then, must unconditionally be the preaching of hope. The two points that determine whether a sermon is in accord with revelation are Christmas and the day of the Lord. If preaching is within these two points, it conforms to revelation. All that is said must always be said between these two points.

2. Church. Barth says that preaching must orient itself solely to baptism as the sign of grace, to the Lord's Supper as the sign of hope, and to the scripture as the record of the truth, and by what God does in this sphere. It is important to note that Barth believes that there must never be in any circumstances the separation between the administration of the sacraments and the proclamation of the gospel. The sacraments bear witness to the content of the event. As a circle has both a center and a periphery, neither is more important than the other, and so both sermon and Sacraments belong to worship in the full sense.

3. Confession. Confession is the response (the confirmation of reception) that we make to what we have heard. When this is done, the church itself is ready for ongoing discharge of the Lord's commission.

4. Ministry. Preaching takes place on the special authority and responsibility of divine calling to ministry in the church. As God's own deed, this institution is always

his own secret, and the called must someday render an account.

5. Holiness. This reference is to the relation between God and us that takes place in the act of preaching. A sermon is always the work of sinners who have neither the ability nor the will for it, but whom God has commanded to do it.

6. Scripture. Preaching as exposition of scripture is in all circumstances under a constraint as regard to both form and content. Preaching must not be a welling up out of our own speech. In both form and content, it must be an exposition of scripture.

7. Originality. Preaching can take place only in personal repentance and thankfulness, and it is thus a free word of the preachers. Holy scripture first has to break through to the preachers. Only then are they in a position to echo it with their own words and their own thinking.

8. Congregation. Preaching aims at the people of a specific time to tell them that their lives have their basis and hope in Jesus Christ. A sermon, therefore, must be very personal. The proclamation is for the hearer.

9. Spirituality. Preaching has to take place in humility and soberness and as the prayer of those who realize that God himself must confess their human word if it is to be God's Word. Preaching, Barth says, must become prayer. It must turn into the seeking and invoking of God, so that ultimately everything depends upon whether God hears and answers our prayers. There is no place, then, for a victorious confidence in the success of our own actions, but only a willingness to open ourselves to heaven and remain open to God, so that God himself can now come to us and give us all things richly. Our

attitudes must be controlled from above: nothing from me, all things from God, no independent achievement, only dependence on God's grace and will.

In chapter 3, "Actual Preparation of the Sermons," Barth says that "the first step in preparing a sermon is thus to realize that we must seek the material for it exclusively in the Old Testament and the New. This alone is the material that we must proclaim to the congregation, for as the community of Jesus Christ it is waiting for the food of Holy Scripture, and nothing else" (p. 92, 93). He then gives some pitfalls and advice on how to avoid those pitfalls in the preparation of sermons or the selection of material for the sermon. For example, we cannot view an address on a theme as having the same rank as a sermon on a text. Barth claims that this is only preliminary, and that, the first step is to read the text. This must be the content of the sermon. Second, when we have read the text, our next step is to inquire into its content. He calls this "the whence and whither" of a text—knowing what is the material both before and after the text to which it is indissolubly associated. Third, we must analyze the text, giving attention to certain features that are in some sense to be viewed as stating in part the purpose of what is said in the text, namely on the proportions of the statements, the order of the concepts, and the drift of the text. Only then should commentaries be used. He discusses at length why this is done and suggests the use of old commentaries as well as new commentaries. Barth recommends, as an afterthought, that should the time for sermon preparation be limited, we must read the text in the original and in Luther's translation.

The next step, Barth says, is *the way of witness* to God's own word. The Bible itself is the witness to God's revelation. God's own Word, Jesus Christ himself, is he that the scriptures testify. Human statements made by the prophets and apostles did not speak of themselves, but spoke the Word of God. The text on which preachers are to preach is part of their train of thought in duty to those whom they proclaim the Word of God. This train of thought is called the way of witness. The witness speaks about that to which it bears witness, though it is not itself the object of its witness. An example is John the Baptist who was not the light, but he bore witness to the light. When he saw Jesus he said, "Behold the lamb of God, which taketh away the sin of the world" (John 1:29).

As regards the content of a sermon, Barth defines it thus: the content of a sermon is a repetition of the *marturia* (a bearing witness) that was written once and for all in the Bible by a person of our own time who offers the repetition, but always with a focus on the apostles and prophets, et cetera. The sermon should never have as its subject familiar truths such as the grandeur of faith, or Christ and country, or known or relatively little-known truths that are sought in the Bible. Instead, it must point to the truth that is absolutely unknown, and it must do so with the hope and prayer that this truth (truth of Jesus Christ) will now itself speak and make itself known through the ministry of this simple reference. Barth explains that behind the biblical text stands the truth that is absolutely unknown to humans but that wills to disclose itself, making itself the absolutely known truth by the calls of the church. To preach is to tread again with the congregation the way of witness taken by the text. Here, Barth confirms, the great burden of the mystery of revelation is lifted from us. What the prophets and apostles heard, we must try to repeat. Barth then gives three technical explanations worthy of note, but it is beyond the scope of this book to include (see *Homiletics* by Karl Barth).

Since the proclamation of the Word is no more than a simple

repetition of the witness that is given to us in scripture, Barth adds, the task takes on a broader dimension. We have to follow this way of witness *into the present.* Preaching is not to be explication alone. It may not be limited to exposition with no regard for the hearers. Every sermon must also take the form of application. An exposition must not turn into a monologue, because there is possibility of a responsive echo from those who hear it. It follows then that there is a need to make a unity out of the duality of exposition and application. Therefore, Barth explains, in describing the relationship between exposition and application in sermon preparation, the following principle holds good: in a sermon, explication must relate to application as a subject does to predicate. As the preacher prepares the sermon, the congregation must be in his or her mind's eye. The preacher will be informed from the emerging insights and associations as he or she prepares the sermon verse by verse. And if the theological exegesis provides an unshakable foundation, the contemporary material will provide the uncertain and relative element in the construction of the sermon.

Barth does suggest a methodological way to proceed. First, write down ideals that come to mind while thinking about the text and cautiously consider the very uncertain and changeable character of the contemporary material, which must be taken into account in our sermon preparation. The people we address are people with all kinds of anxieties and needs. It is in this concrete situation of their earth condition and situation that the call of Jesus Christ comes to them as people of the present age. Preachers themselves belong to the congregation, and so they must never feel superior to the congregation but must also hear the Word of God. Recognition of this situation of the preachers is the basis prerequisite for the proper application of the Word, which at the same time can never cease to be explication.

Each word that is to be proclaimed to the listeners must become a word that is specifically and decisively addressed to our own present. What the text has to say may be said unconditional, even if it costs the preacher his or her neck. Openness to the text and the courage to proclaim it is what must be emphasized. The Word of scripture alone bears the responsibility. Guard against the intrusion into the text of thoughts we feel are associated with the reality of people today, warns Barth when in fact it is not in the text itself but that we think we must unconditionally bring into the sermon because of certain intoxication with the beauty of the thought. Barth explains that we too willingly confuse the beautiful thoughts of our self-seeking egos with the thoughts of the text that are usually less comfortable and less in keeping with the thinking of the age. Arbitrarily intruded material must be excluded. It is important, therefore, to reexamine the material in light of the text, putting it through a second filter, so to speak. Regarding the difficulty between explication and application—namely in the tension between closeness to life and closeness to the text, and humility or caution in the face of it—Barth believes that this tension is indissoluble but that both must always be taken into account. There is a slight tilt in favor of the relation between love of God and love of neighbor, he responds. For in preaching, he says, it is better to be too close to the text than to be too thematic or too much in keeping with the times. Of two evils, it is better here to choose the lesser. Notwithstanding, Barth lists three warnings with explanations that arise in this connection.

Next, the sermon itself is written. It is part of the sanctification of the preacher to feel bound once and for all to this rule. Each sermon should be ready for print, as it was, before it is delivered. By this rule, no one is condemned, but we must set ourselves the task of considering what is right for one who is not a prophet but must prepare sermons with prayer and toil. The sermon demands an orderly language that is appropriate from the standpoint of content as well as expression. Form and content are not to be separated in preaching. The right form is part of the right content, affirms Barth.

Regarding the actual execution of the sermon, Barth recommends the following points, in summary: (a) *Totality*. The totality (whole) of the sermon is constituted by the totality of the given text. The unity lies in the text itself and should find expression in the sermon, which follows the movement of the text. (b) *Introduction*. Basically, the sermon should not have an introduction, and only one kind of legitimate introduction is conceivable. When a scripture reading precedes the sermon, a link can be made with this, so that in some sense the sermon proper begins with a pre-sermon consisting of a brief analysis of the lesson that leads up to the real sermon. This is the only possible form of introduction. All others are to be rejected in principle. (c) *Parts*. Barth believes that the sermon has to be a body, not with parts but with members. He questions the parts because in a homily the proper way is to construct the body of the sermon in repetition of the text's own rhythm, with regard to the proportions distinguished by exegesis. (d) *Conclusion*. As with rejecting the special introduction, no independent conclusion can be drawn. The sermon needs to end with the exposition.

Knowing why Barth says this is important. Here is a brief summary of the psychological (practical) reasons he offers against such introduction. (1) The course of worship itself is the introduction to the sermon, its climax. The act of proclamation should begin at once. Any additional introduction is a waste of time. Too much precious time is wasted by intellectual wit and cleverness (or gymnastics of this kind). Twenty to twenty-five minutes may often be spent on preliminaries before coming to the main point. (2) The greater part of all introductions does not introduce. It distracts our thoughts from the Word of God. Instead of leading in, it leads out. At the beginning of a sermon, the listeners are still in a state of suspense and attentiveness. If the preacher first converses about something else—maybe something very interesting—it may well happen that one or the other of them will be completely turned off when a switch is finally made to the real matter at hand. (3) What meaning does an introduction have for serious listeners who want to hear a call from God and are ready for it? They will be disappointed in their purpose, and their frustration will block their hearing of the message.

Barth asks, "What is it that the introduction usually contains?" Then he gives four very good stances for introductions but turns around and cuts the legs out from under them. He remarks that when the Word has found an entrance into a person, then God has worked the miracle—he alone, without any preparation or assistance from us. We have to simply approach people knowing that there is nothing in them that we can address—that we can put in touch with the divine. We have to simply adopt the attitude of the messenger who does not have to create a mood for the message. No doubt, Barth believes all this seems to be wildly destructive of the little garden of our sermon out of which we hoped to pluck so many blooms!

Preaching cannot try to relate to the divine within us, says Barth. The miracle must always take place from above. The human listener must be seen and addressed as Adam after the fall, but in light of the fact that this listener has been called in Christ by baptism. In baptism, however, we have received only the promise, never a point of contact. We have no need to build a slowly ascending ramp because there is no height that we have to reach. Something has to come down from above. This can happen only when the Bible speaks from the very outset. We have then done what we could.

The proper way to construct the corpus of the sermon is in repetition of the text own rhythm and with due regard to the proportions discerned by exegesis. In such repetition, we need not deal with the passage schematically, verse by verse, as in the work of preparation. The decisive point at which to begin will be the middle or the end of the verse or passage. The aim of the sermon should not be that people receive a few thoughts but that they open the Bible and note the way of witness that it takes.

What about conclusions? You guessed it! Barth rejects the special introduction, and so there can be no independent conclusion; the sermon has to end with the exposition. If a summary is needed, it is already too late to give it; the mischief has already been done. A theoretical sermon cannot be made more practical by a concluding application. Motivating is especially dangerous and seductive, says Barth. As surely as this may be done, he warns against it as a method. The sermon must be worship, but as a whole and not merely at the end. If it is so only at the end, it is no longer credible, he explains. An important, comforting, and critical little word is the *amen* with which we confess what we have said before God. *Amen* may be a comfort to us after what has been said in weakness. Every sermon thus closes on both a comforting and an unsettling note.

Barth concludes by saying that if a question is raised in conclusion, it should be meant only as a proclamation and never as a new problem relating to a questionable opinion. Barth now mentions free prayer after the sermon. He says that it is mere babble that gives the impression the preacher is not prepared.

That should not be. And as regards the reading of the sermon, Barth says that the main point is that what is done should be right and responsible, and that it is not out of keeping with the "good news" that the sermon be read. In conclusion, *Homiletics* presents Barth's lecture materials from seminars in Bonn from 1932 to 1933 and has an astonishing relevance even today. His doctrine of preaching will undoubtedly find grateful readers and evoke joy and courage for the proclamation of the gospel. I encourage the reading of his book for further information for those called to preach to gain new insights on the proclamation of the gospel.

In his book *Black Preaching: The Recovery of a Powerful Art,*[15] Dr. Henry H. Mitchell explains the significance and importance of culture in understanding the language and style of preaching, and especially black preaching, that arose out of the African Traditional Religion. He explains the term "black hermeneutics" as it applies to black religious communication of the absolute truth of God as revealed in the scriptures. He states the reason why religious communication of blacks has survived. The new hermeneutics of the Germans had nothing over black hermeneutics because the latter operated on two very sound principles. He then stresses the importance of spirituals as being the code language of the gospel of self-liberation and other messages. A standard mixture of practical mysticism and pragmatically told renditions of Bible stories has helped black preaching retain the interest of its audience.

Mitchell tells of the history of black preaching and how the preaching tradition of blacks developed over this period out of the black experience of slavery and oppression. Black preachers arose out of the ranks of the Methodists and Baptists, and he states the reason why. Also, he gives reasons why the early black preachers preached more to whites than blacks. In early stages, a visible black congregation was unthinkable. He discusses the style and content of early black preaching and also the hazards faced by early black preachers. The power of black preaching can be seen by the fact that the black belief system of folk Christianity has kept its believers alive and coping. The reason was a sound theological message that comes alive in a meaningful experience for the hearer.

Early black preachers were not free to study, explains Mitchell, and therefore lacked formal training. However, Mitchell points out the fact that they spoke and worked so fruitfully without formal training is evident that God bypassed white academic structures to give America a corps of black preachers with deep insight and relevance. He then explains the failures and tragedies of black people who slavishly followed the white man's pattern of culture and the resultant stereotype least admirable in the black man's culture. Notwithstanding, he notes that an education adds to the irreplaceable factors of worship to a great preacher and native gifts chargeable only to God.

Mitchell elaborately explains why the black Bible is a living epistle of God's way and will for everyday problems of black people. The preacher therefore avoids focus on scientific-historical truths and focuses rather on truth for the life of the spirit. He explains how this is done effectively through biblical scholarship, adding that imagination and biblical facts are part of this tradition. Storytelling, he explains, is not "narrative theology" that leads to the expression of doctrine in stories, as seen in the black tradition. Rather, the black Bible story is a work of art in which the storyteller plays all the roles and makes the story live.

All people worship God in the language in which they are born, says Mitchell. He suggests that black preachers (or teachers), who have struggled so hard to speak proper English, retain some of their native tongue with which to establish identity with their congregations (or students). Black preaching requires the use of black language. He then explains the why, what, and how of speaking black English as it relates to black preaching, as well as the cultural identity needed for a black-culture church. Educated black clergy, he adds, need to be linguistically flexible to communicate with most congregations at most times and in most circumstances.

Mitchell describes at length the personal style of the black preacher: the use of mannerisms, tone, rhythm, call and response and repetition, role playing and storytelling, subjectivity and rhetorical flair, slow delivery, aphorisms, and hesitation. He discusses black dialogue between preacher and congregation (as an element of call and response), black dialogue and social distance (there must be closeness of preacher and people), black dialogue and activism (social activism is encouraged), black dialogue and contagion (the use of the stimulator or initiator of the dialogue), and the black dialogue (as resource in black preaching). Without dialogue, there is no distinctly black sermon. Proclamation with power requires dialogue.

Mitchell says that the routes by which the sermon arrives at the celebrative conclusion are as many and varied as the preachers themselves, the various audiences, and the dialogue between them occurring in each of the sermons. He discusses introductions by saying that there are two types: the self-introduction of the preacher to a new audience, and the introduction of the sermon itself. He also describes praise speeches and their significance as honor to the sacred pulpit of another and for reasons of cultural momentum. He discusses the three main types of sermons common in the black pulpit: textual, expositional, and narrative. Then he discusses at length celebration, and according to Mitchell, it is one aspect of the sermon that most nearly deserves to be called typically black. He describes that celebration is a necessity, but not to canonize a culturally quaint habit; rather, it is to theologize concerning this important aspect of black preaching.

Finally, he adds, "The goodness of God must not be a distant theory; it must be a present fact, which to experience is to celebrate." To engage in the business of black preaching without the theological assumptions that underlie the black tradition is either to be wanting in sincerity or to labor without support, says Mitchell. Even though this book is of special interest to blacks, anyone called to preach can learn from its contents and adapt the message for his or her particular situation or congregational needs.

PART 3

PREACHERS AND PREACHING

INTRODUCTION

Preachers today are not Old Testament prophets or New Testament apostles. Unless one would be guilty of both presumption and anachronism, one must constantly keep in mind the great difference between preachers then and preachers now. Preachers today do not receive their messages directly from God the way the prophets did. Neither can preachers today claim with the apostles that they were eyewitnesses (2 Pet. 1:16; Luke 1:2). And yet provided their sermons are biblical, preachers today may also claim to bring the Word of God.[1] Hence, we shall now focus on the preparation and delivery of sermons.

SERMON PREPARATION

A sermon is different from a lecture, an essay, a theological dissertation, or a speech on any topic because of the uniqueness of the sermon. The uniqueness of the sermon is due to the creative touch that makes of scattered truths and miscellaneous insights a living and convincing unity of ideas. In a sermon, there is trust that God has something to say to the people. The sermon is also different in that it is the product of the processes of homiletics (the study of sermon preparation), exegesis ("to lead out of"—a narration or explanation), and hermeneutics (the science of expounding or interpreting what a passage of scripture says). The sermon should bring good tidings or good news. Unlike a lecture, an essay, a theological dissertation, or a speech on any topic, the sermon is a message of God to men to communicate divine truths with a view to persuade. The sermon is therefore divine truths spoken with a view of persuasion.

In planning the sermon, the idea, subject, and the text should relate to each other. Well-determined goals of preaching in general, and the aims of preaching in particular, should be a basis for finding sermon subjects. Two fundamental objectives should always be kept in mind and followed. First, every sermon should be carefully and definitely aimed. Second, it should be remembered that great ideas of text suggest great subjects or themes. The preacher must be deeply aware of people's need of instruction as to the worth of a person's soul and the sacredness of human personality. All these and many other religious matters enter into the choice of preaching themes. There are important moral and social issues—local, national, and international—that affect people living together and the lifting up of their personal lives. The purpose and aim of the sermon are to throw light on life, religion, and the human problems of the world in our times. The sermon must answer people's questions in light of the meaning of religion. Those questions are answered by reference to experience, biblical interpretation, and literature—all are important records of human experience. Thus, the idea may be from the secular world (newspaper, television, radio, or experience), but its truth will be biblically supported by the text (scripture). The theme should come from the text itself and lead to three or four points. Every point should lead back to the idea, and every sub-point should lead to the one it follows. Good illustrations will obviously be needed to capture the people's attention.

Every sermon must have some plan of organization. Constructing the plan is next to the final step in the preparation. The general plan includes the introduction, the body, and the conclusion. This part of the sermon is often called the outline. The introduction is sometimes compared to the porch of a house through which occupants or visitors enter. They are there for only a short while. Its purpose is to capture the interest of the listeners and prepare them for understanding the main theme that is to be presented in the body. Then follows the development in which the main theme is explored and elaborated. Finally, the conclusion should have the force of application and appeal. The recapitulation brings the composition of the sermon to a close. The conclusion reinforces the points.

An outline is desirable for preachers and their listeners because it largely determines how much meaning the sermon will have for the people. It is by the outline that most people grasp and understand the sermon. Many may remember only the outline—if it is clearly stated. The heading or topic constitute, for them, the minister's message. Every sermon must have some plan of organization. Usually the plan includes the introduction, the body or argument, and the conclusion. Within this pattern, each sermon has its own specific plan, which is the skeleton or framework of ideas that make up the sermon. This planning gives order and definiteness to the sermon, not only from the standpoint of construction, but the hearers may more readily understand it as well. With better understanding comes greater retention of the message.

There are three advantages of an outline for the preacher: (1) An outline enables the preacher to give structure to his or her message. (2) An outline enables the preacher to move logically toward an effective climax. (3) An outline enables the preacher to better summarize what has been said for a final impression upon the listener. Subsequently, there are three advantages of an outline for the listener: (1) A clear outline allows the listener to follow the logical unfolding of the message as it is delivered. (2) The outline gives a sense of pace to the sermon that the listener can follow. (3) The outline allows the listener to see the points moving toward the climax, giving a sense of expectancy and anticipation to the listeners.

To some, sermon preparation is an art, and to others it is a science. Then there are some who view the sermon as an art and a science. We should continue to educate ourselves to appreciate the value of good sermon preparation. Always be willing and ready to learn methods that made others effective and that may assist you in your quest to be God's best at your calling.

SERMON DELIVERY

There is another book that I would like to bring to the attention of the one called to preach. It is a book that can become a powerful tool in the improvement of the preacher's sermon delivery. It will prove extremely helpful to those who have formal training in sermon delivery and to those who have not. In explaining its contents, I will comment on just how helpful the book will be to those seeking insight on sermon delivery.

Dr. Jerry Vines' book *A Guide to Effective Sermon Delivery, Moody Press* deals with some vital areas of sermon delivery: psychological aspects of sermon delivery, mechanical aspects of sermon delivery, spiritual aspects of sermon delivery, and rhetorical aspects of sermon delivery.

Psychological Aspects of Sermon Delivery

Vines' psychological aspects of sermon delivery make one aware of the need to effectively communicate the prepared sermon to the congregation. Vines is right in his assessment of the present generation, in that our generation is witnessing a communication revolution, and we preachers are no longer allowed to be shabby in our presentation. Realizing this will help one to do one's very best without compromising effective communication. Effective delivery of the message of the gospel to our generation is vital, especially in light of what Vines calls the "swift-moving images of the television screen." Therefore, it is imperative that preachers are more concerned about their sermon delivery in light of the communication revolution. Emotionally, one may feel challenged to do one's best. Personally, I am affected because of this awareness. I must therefore continue to improve in all areas of effective sermon delivery, using all my God-given gifts to his glory, as the one called to preach will feel inclined to do.

Vines' psychological aspects of sermon delivery affected me by informing me of the need to be aware of feedback from the audience—there is audience inter-stimulation and response. Preaching is enhanced through the realization and experience of participation in the preaching event as a whole. Also, on a person note, preaching is enhanced because my attitude when I am preaching is one of "we" and not "you." I am included in my preaching.

The Word is to me and for me. The one called to preach will do well if this is remembered. The preacher should be aware of the audience response and the need to be an audience-centered preacher. Preaching should never be a monologue. We should preach to the audience and make eye contact for effective preaching.

Mechanical Aspects of Sermon Delivery

The study of Vines' mechanical aspects of sermon delivery had helped me better perform the task of preaching. Vines details several areas in mechanical aspects of sermon delivery to understand the importance of techniques: relaxing, breathing, articulating, integrating, and improving the voice and caring for the voice.

Relaxing. Vines points out that unusual tension will affect the voice and subsequently the total personality. Without relaxation, the voice cannot be well coordinated. I have addressed negative attitudes that cause too much tension in my speaking and have become more effective in preaching.

Breathing. Proper breathing relieves muscle tension. Having sufficient breath to complete our sentences without gulping or losing the closing words, and to amplify our voices during the sentence, is consciously controlled. Vines suggests propelling the breath in a relaxed manner and completing each sentence in the most effective way. I have found this suggestion to be most effective. Also, speaking in a natural tone of voice, being natural, is very effective.

Articulation. Forming the sounds that characterize good speech is articulation and is synonymous with enunciation. Articulation is important for listeners' understanding. Equally important is that articulation is a key ingredient in achieving maximum relaxation during sermon delivery. I feel less tension in my voice when I speak and consciously make an effort to properly articulate words. Practicing making the tongue more flexible has helped me very much. Also, pronunciation and enunciation are generally extremely important in our culture, particularly in the preaching profession.

Integrating. Good breathing and good articulation are not enough. Communication is hindered when we speak too quickly or too slowly. A sermon should be delivered with excitement and vigor, but not in haste. I have worked on the rate and pace of my sermon, and the delivery of my sermons has improved. Using pause and variety in volume have been of great benefit to me. I am still working on pitch and inflection, and I do stay away from monotony.

Improving the Voice and Caring for the Voice. In an effort to improve the voice, I have listened to myself on tape and have listened to other effective preachers. After studying myself and other good preachers, I see the need for improvement. This is good. Vines suggests a regular program of self-improvement. Reading aloud, he says, is a good way to improve sermon delivery. I love reading, and so this will be the best self-improvement plan for me to naturally stick with. I encourage the one called to preach to read a wide variety of books.

I realize the voice to be of great importance in the communication of God's Word. Precaution and care are needed to protect the voice from vocal disorders. Wrong force, wrong pitch, and wrong breathing cause vocal disturbance. Therefore, I closely observe what may be the cause of any throat irritation, such as hoarseness or throat fatigue, so that immediate remedies may be applied. I try to avoid causes of voice problems; for example, eating before preaching is a no-no. The result of studying Vines' mechanical aspects of sermon delivery has produced an increased awareness of the necessity of good vocal hygiene.

Spiritual Aspects of Sermon Delivery

One thing that Vines says in spiritual aspects of sermon delivery that really hit home with me is his conviction that the spiritual aspects of sermon delivery is most crucial. I concur wholeheartedly. I am affected by the conviction that the Spirit's anointing is everything. Vines says that if the Spirit's anointing is lacking, none of the other aspects of delivery can make up for its absence. I live by the conviction that without the blessing of the Holy Spirit upon my preaching, my sermon will have no effect at all. There must be heart in preaching to stir others to action.

Vines' spiritual aspects of sermon delivery affect me in a very special way. I realize that preaching is effective only when accompanied by the Holy Spirit's power. I desire God's presence whenever I preach (in preparation and delivery). Vines says that there must be cooperation between the Spirit of God and the minister of God. An awareness of this partnership brings about confidence and assurance as the preacher stands to preach. Whenever I preach, this is what I feel, and my preaching is enhanced by God's power. When the anointing of the Spirit of God is upon my preaching, I know in my spirit that God is at work. Vines explained this well in spiritual aspects of sermon delivery, and what he said enhanced my understanding of the evidence of the Spirit's power in preaching, thus greatly affecting my dependence upon the Holy Spirit. The anointing of the Spirit will be discussed further under the heading "The Preacher's Authority."

Rhetorical Aspects of Sermon Delivery

It should be preachers' desire to preach effectively and to improve so that they are the very best that they are capable of becoming. To this end, rhetorical aspects of sermon delivery may help.

Rhetoric is generally defined as the art of using words effectively in speaking to influence or persuade others. It is the art of ready utterance, appropriate expression, and moving appeal. The preacher must convey the Word of God in language that is clear and understandable. The use of words can enhance or weaken the effectiveness of the preacher's sermon. As a guideline, the preacher's words must be clear, interest-provoking, and forceful. But be careful. There is always the danger that too much attention to rules and norms for delivery can cause rigidity in one's delivery. Too much attention to the art of rhetoric can produce a kind of unreality about your preaching. Remember to be yourself! Preach in your natural voice, utilizing your own personality.

Dramatic technique can strengthen the preacher's sermon delivery. The preacher must use words that can be understood at the moment of hearing by the listeners. The spoken style must make use of suspense and climax to build a sense of expectancy for the listeners. More repetition and restatement may be used to ensure that the listeners have clearly heard what the preacher wants to say. The preacher, in his or her oral communication, may use comparisons and contrasts for vividness. The use of illustrations will cause greater retention for the hearers. In the spoken language, figurative speech must be used to produce pictures in the minds of the listeners. The oral style must also include more questions and personal elements of address for rapport with the audience. The message must be presented with rhythm and smoothness. The preacher must deliver the sermon in words that convey excitement, interest, expectancy, and eagerness.

Use words appropriate to the occasion; know the occasion, the audience, and the type of message to be delivered. In other words, choose words fitting the time, place, and purpose of the gathering. Do not use the technical terminology you learned in college or seminary in the pulpit. Your purpose is not to be impressive but to communicate. Again, know your audience or congregation—use one level of word selection for children or young adults and another level for that of senior adults. Words do not have to be long and complicated to be effective. Use simple words that even children can understand, use clear words that give meaning correctly, and avoid words that give a general meaning that can refer to a variety of qualities or feelings. Bible language can be hard to understand sometimes. Your job is to teach the people the meaning of Bible terms in words that are simple and easy to understand.

PERSUASION

The preacher must use techniques of persuasion. Persuasion refers to all the ethical methods the preacher may use in his preaching to induce people to make the right decisions and do the right things. The one called to preach must preach for a verdict. The intent here is to bring the listeners to a point of decision that will eternally change their destiny, not merely the influencing of behavior but ultimately the changing of character. In persuasion, most advertising appeals use four basic methods that may be utilized by the preacher.

1. *The appeal to virtue*. Such a device calls attention to the person's interest in some desirable, achievable goal.
2. *The poison device*. This is where failure to use the desirable product is associated with everything undesirable, objectionable, and harmful.
3. *The testimonial*. This seeks to induce the acceptance or rejection of a product on the basis of persons with reputation and personal appeal.
4. *Group pressure*. This combines the other three and operates by means of group pressure.

The preacher must penetrate defenses, break down patterns of thoughts, and bring about changes in the lives of his or her listeners. The preacher's goal is this: that the minds of those who listen be convinced, that their emotions be stirred, and that their wills be activated. But do not take the position that any method of influence is good if it has positive results. The end does not justify the means.

Even though persuasion is what preaching is all about (the particular words used are to persuade or induce one by words to believe), we are to be persuaders, not manipulators. Note the following faulty approaches.

A. "I won't try to persuade at all" (the Christian is commanded by the Lord Jesus Christ Himself to win people).
B. "Show them only the silver lining" (shading the truth and failure to present the total picture is untrue to the Christian gospel).

Methods of manipulation that promise worldly success are unworthy of the sincere Christian preacher who desires to bring individuals to faith in Christ and to changed lifestyles. The preacher must never seek to persuade others to make themselves appear to be successful.

The great Aristotle was persuaded by three factors: ethos, logos, and pathos.

1. *Ethos* means the impression the preacher makes upon his or her audience. Preachers must live the messages they preach. The listener must get the impression of modesty, sincerity, humility, and genuineness to respond favorably to what preachers say.
2. *Logos* refers to the use of logic and formal methods of persuasion. The elements of analogy, induction,

deduction, and testimony are the formal methods of argument.

3. *Pathos* is the appeal to the emotions. Never appeal to feelings exclusively because they are baser motives; rather, appeal to the highest longings and aspirations of humans. On the basis of Aristotle's divisions, persuasive techniques may fall into three categories: personal appeal, logical argument, and emotional appeal.

Dr. Charles W. Koller, in "How to Preach Without Notes,"‡ says there are seven appeals to the heart.

1. *The appeal to altruism.* A benevolent regard for the interests of others.
2. *The appeal to aspiration.* The universal hunger for spiritual happiness or a sense of completeness.
3. *The appeal to curiosity.* The susceptibility to that which appears novel, unfamiliar, or mysterious.
4. *The appeal to duty.* The divine urge to do a thing because it is right, or to refrain from a thing because it is wrong.
5. *The appeal to fear.* Fear of punishment.
6. *The appeal to love.* Love of self, love of others, or love of God.
7. *The appeal to reason.* An appeal to intelligent self-interest.

If used prayerfully, these persuasive techniques can add much to the preacher's message. Those called to preach should study them diligently and prayerfully as they seek to incorporate them into the sermons according to the will of God.

---

‡ *The Basic Appeals in Biblical Preaching*, third printing (Baker Books, 1998), 108–112.

METHODS OF DELIVERY

There are four basic methods of delivering a message: manuscript, memory, impromptu, and extemporaneous. There may be other types of delivering a message, but these are the basic types. Preachers will have to develop their own techniques in order to find out which works best for them.

1. *The manuscript method of delivery* is when the preacher reads the manuscript word for word. This method usually lacks the true, heartfelt meaning initially intended and ends up being monotonous.

2. *The memory method of delivery* is when the sermon is written out in full, committed to memory, and then delivered without any reference to manuscript or notes. The main drawback to this method is the danger of memory lapse, which could cause hesitations throughout the sermon.

3. *The impromptu method of delivery* is when the preacher speaks from the top of his or her head with no preparation. No effective expository sermon can be delivered this way.

4. *The extemporaneous method of delivery* is when the preacher waits until the moment of delivery before the ideas are formed into actual words. The logical flow

of main ideas has to be clearly established. The main drawback to this method is rambling, but this method may be the most commonly used among expository preachers.

The great preachers of the past and present have used the extemporaneous method and have followed four basic steps. First, they organize and outline well. Second, they memorize main points and reference them in the scriptures. Third, they overlearn their material. Fourth, they saturate themselves with the message. Preachers go over the message again and again in their heads, up until the sermon itself. If you preach extemporaneously, do not be disturbed if you forget some things. If an impression is so weak you could not remember it, then it was probably best left out of the sermon. Preachers will have to determine for themselves the best method of sermon proclamation. Do not allow your fears to hinder you from giving each method a try.

THE CREATIVE PROCESS

Sermon preparation and delivery are acts of creativity, born of the Holy Spirit and the life and labors of the one called to preach. Almost every person involved in some kind of creative endeavor has experienced a sudden burst of illumination or insight. One may work at a hard question, and nothing good is accomplished at the first attack. Then one takes a rest for a short or longer period and sits down anew to work. During the first half hour, as before nothing happens, and suddenly the decisive idea presents itself.

There are four phases in the creative process.

1. **Preparation**. This is a time of sustained preliminary labor. During this stage, you expose yourself to the widest possible range of information about the subject.
2. **Incubation**. This is the time given to germination and maturing of the main idea. A time of rest and recreation is needed. This gives the unconscious mind the opportunity to perceive on its own. This rest or change releases a person from intensive effort and allows the creative impulse free rein to express itself.
3. **Illumination**. This is the moment of insight. This dynamic process comes out of periods of study, matures

in the hidden subjective levels of thought, and springs into life with startling suddenness.

4. **Verification**. The creative idea must then be developed and elaborated in terms of the surrounding context. The inspired concept must be checked with the available facts that have been brought forth in the previous preparation. This enables one to verify and authenticate the accuracy of the creative idea.

The preacher must go through preparation. The steps involved in the exposition of a passage (discussed later) must be carried out. Time must be spent in the process of organizing the scripture passage. The subconscious mind must be given the opportunity to work on the context that has been assembled. As the preacher meditates on his or her scripture passage, he or she is preparing the way for the creative process. The preacher can do this as he or she walks, jogs, or drives. The moment of illumination in your sermon preparation may come during the day, away from your preparation. When the creative moment comes, be sure to record what you receive. The concept of incubation may be another way of expressing the role the Holy Spirit plays in sermon preparation. The one who inspired the scriptures must also give the one who would preach them understanding and insight into their meaning. The Holy Spirit must place in the bonds of the preacher the keys that actually unlock their meaning and provide their application. Again, when the creative moment comes, quickly verify its accuracy in relation to the facts you have found in your expository investigation.

THE PROCESS OF EXPOSITION

The process of exposition is the whole process of analyzing a passage of scripture in preparing an expository sermon. The scripture passage has to be dissected into its various parts as if it was, for example, a fully functional automobile engine before, and to see it as an exploded view of all the parts of the motor in order to determine how the parts come together to make a functional engine. While the automobile engine is a minute illustration, hopefully it serves as a simile to view how exposition involves critical explanation or interpretation of the meaning of a scripture passage, which in turn involves leading out of the passage what the passage actually says. In exegesis, the intent is to view all of the parts of the scriptural passage which make up the whole to discern the meaning it is intended to convey. The in-depth process is known as the induction method.

Induction is the process of inference by which we arrive at a mere general truth from a particular set of facts. Induction is concerned about collating, analyzing, and observing everything in the passage as it relates to the subject being treated. In exposition, there is a threefold process: investigation, interpretation, and application.

1. *Investigation* is the reading of the scripture passage to determine what it says and what it means. In investigation, we are to read, reread, and read again and again. The scripture passage must be read prayerfully, carefully, imaginatively, and obediently to the Bible truths found. As you read the Bible, look for the theme and main points using the following tools: who, what, when, where, how, and why. Also, look for repetitions of terms, phrases, clauses, or sentences, and observe transitional words that indicate the introduction of a new thought or the conclusion of a previous one.

2. *Interpretation* is the next step in the process. After investigation, we should know what the passage says. Interpretation will answer the next question of what the passage means. This is where one tries to determine the core of the sentences: the main subject, the main verb, and the main object of each sentence in the preaching passage(s). Then one does a textual recreation, where all the sentences are diagrammed. Such clues as repetitions, comparisons, and progressions are indented, underlined, or circled and tied together by lines drawn to get a picture of the entire passage. This procedure helps in seeing the unifying theme and supporting divisions and shows the repetitions that occur.

Next, a word study is done. Through careful study of the words and the relationships of the words, the literal meaning of the Bible text can be determined. Sometimes the Bible language is to be understood figuratively. Observe the following figures of speech that occur in the Bible: similes, metaphors, paradoxes, and hyperboles. They can change your understanding as you interpret the meaning of the passage.

Next, study the context or that part of a discourse in

which the passage occurs. The context guides us in explaining the meaning of the passage. Then gather the historical data (the historical setting, the customs of the times, the political and religious conditions) for an adequate interpretation of a scripture passage. Do cross-reference work to allow the scripture to interpret itself. Doing parallel studies will greatly aid the understanding of the scriptures.

Then, the theological significant of the passage should be determined. This is mandatory to good exposition. Studying the theological significance of our passage of scripture will bring you in contact with truths of the passage that can be related in a practical way to real people in a real world. Then consult commentaries, but only after you have lingered over the Bible passage and deciphered the truths and meanings for yourself. Learn to bring every commentary to the judgment of scripture.

The last suggestion of interpretation is to apply proper principles of interpretation. First, the *ethnic principle* states that the entire human race is divided into three categories: the new, the gentile, and the church. All scripture is addressed to one of these three categories. Although all scripture applies to us, not all is necessarily addressed to us. Second, the *first mention principle* suggests that very often subjects in the Bible are given one comprehensive treatment somewhere in the Bible— for example, love in 1 Corinthians 13. Third, there is also the principle of *proportionate mention,* which suggests that the amount of space given in scripture to a particular theme needs to be noted for the magnification of those truths that scripture magnifies. Fourth, the principle of *repeated mention,* which is found on the recognition that when a subject is repeated again and again, added details will be included. Fifth is the *gap principle,* which if understood can shed light upon the meaning of a passage. On occasion, God ignores certain periods of time and leaps over many centuries without comment. Look for such gaps that are messianic in nature, and your interpretation of scripture will be invaluably aided. The sixth principle is called the *salvation/ fellowship* principle. Scripture distinguishes between being in God's family and God's fellowship. This principle is valuable in matters of interpretation, and it helps in avoiding the contradiction of fundamental truths in the scriptures. Seventh on the list is the threefold principle that is a helpful principle in interpretation of God's great truth of salvation. The *salvation principle* is presented in a threefold way: justification (I have been saved), sanctification (I am being saved), and glorification (I will be saved). Last but not least on the list of principles is the principle of *recurrence*. Here is where God's Word may state a subject again from a different viewpoint, with a different purpose. All the above principles will help determine what the scripture passage means and will allow us to move into the third and final step of the process of exposition.

3. *Application* is determining what the passage tells me, and the people to whom I preach, to do. After being faced with the truths found in God's Word, self-application is needed. I must face God's truth in my own heart and life. Next is application to the people. Bible truths must be brought to bear in a practical way upon the lives of our people. The message must be organized in such a way that a definite application is made along the way. We can do this by asking questions and answering them, but we must apply the message to real people, in real places, who have real problems or needs. Dig into

the Word and draw from there practical truths that can touch your people where they hurt.

We must link what we have found in the scriptures to life situations, circumstances encountered by our people, and needs that cry out for solutions in their daily existence. Every interpretation we draw from scripture must have application to the current problems of people. As we do our expository work, we should ask ourselves, "What is the human condition to which the timely truths of this message may be addressed?" As expositors move through the main points of their sermons, they will state them in such a way as to apply to the needs they have mentioned in their introductions. As expositor preachers put together their conclusions, they will gather all the practical ingredients of the scripture passages from which they preach. They will apply scripture passages from which they preach. They will apply scripture definitely and directly to their hearers in one final, stirring appeal to their hearts.

The role of the Holy Spirit in Bible preaching solves many problems. He arouses in the listeners' hearts a deep desire to know the truth, to accept the adequacy of the work of Christ, and the desirability of salvation through him. The power of the Holy Spirit makes preaching effective and applicable; it takes the preaching of the Word and applies timeless truths in a practical way to the lives of those helped. The Holy Spirit powerfully applies the Word when the preacher preaches. The expositor process is consummated in the delivery of the expository sermon by the power of the Holy Spirit.

In summary, the fundamental step in the process of scripture exposition is investigation. Investigation answers the question, "What does the scripture passage really say?" There is only one way to determine this: read the passage. Second in the process of scripture exposition is interpretation. What does the passage mean? The purpose is to find the exact meaning of the scripture passage. Third, application is where Bible truths are applied to the daily lives of those who listen to sermon. "What does the passage tell me to do, and what does it tell those to whom I preach to do?"

EXPOSITORY PREACHING

In expository preaching, the main points should be drawn from the passage. The object of these points, or divisions, in the message is to make clear the central ideal of your text. Expository preaching is exposing the scriptures. First is the analysis. The purpose is to discover the basic content and progression of thought. Second is the exposition. The analysis has to be amplified and enlarged by interpretation and illustration. Third is the sermon itself. The expository sermon, based upon careful analysis and exposition, takes the material, arranges the content in logical order so that the outline can be constructed from it, makes practical application of the materials and ideas to the lives of the people, is properly illustrated, and drives the message home in the conclusion.

The expository sermon is the unfolding of the truth contained in a passage longer than two or three consecutive verses. As a rule, the structure of the expository sermon follows the order of the ideas in the passage, but not slavishly. The emphasis is on the preaching, not the exposition. Although expository preaching is to preach "from the Bible," the heart of the message should be about God in Christ. If one has a sufficient reason for transposing the order of the materials, or omitting some of them altogether, there is nothing in homiletics to hamper one's freedom. The emphasis is upon the freedom of pulpit expositors to deal with the Bible as it seems to them in view of their ability and their people's highest welfare.

Finally, expository preachers have a powerful ally as they seek to creatively communicate God's Word to the layperson or anyone in the pew. The role of the Holy Spirit in Bible preaching solves many problems. The Holy Spirit takes the preaching of the Word and applies timeless truths in a practical way to the lives of those helped.

TYPES OF SERMONS

The one called to preach may choose from a wide variety of sermon types, but the expository sermon is the most common. Listed below are some common types of sermons, with a brief explanation of each.

1. An *expository sermon* secures its major and first sub-points primarily from the text, makes plain what the Bible says, and gives good application to the lives of the hearers. This sermon is based upon a passage from the Bible, and the actual meaning of the Bible passage must be related to the immediate and general context of the passage. The expository sermon gathers the truth of the passage around a central theme. In short, an expository sermon is one that expounds a passage of scripture, organizes it around a central theme and main points, and then decisively applies its message to the hearers.

2. The *topical sermon* is one that owes its form to the unfolding of the truth wrapped up in the title. It secures its points primarily from the title or topic, or it is built around some particular subject or idea. The topical sermon, then, is one in which a subject is deduced from the text but discussed independently from it. Beyond

suggesting the subject, no further use is made of the text.

3. The *textual sermon* is a blend of the previous two. It secures its major points from the text and its minor points from the title or from any other source. The textual sermon is considered to be a careful treatment of a short passage of scripture (two verses or less). When the sermon is textual in fact as in name, the minister is interpreting the truth enshrined in the text. In the technical sense, it is one in which the structure follows the order of the ideas in the text. The textual sermon is one in which the text is the theme, and the parts of the text are the divisions of the discourse and are used as a line of suggestions. This sermon method uses the text in a manner similar to the analytical sermon, which will be explained later.

4. In the case of the *inferential sermon,* the development consists of a series of inference drawn from the text. This method is identical to the synthetic method, which will be explained later.

5. The *biblical sermon* is considered to be the treatment of three or more verses of scripture. It is an interpretation of divine truth and human duty as revealed in the scriptures.

6. The *analytical sermon* is when the order of the points is the same in the sermon and in the text. The preacher says exactly what the text says or expresses, although he or she may not always say it in the same words. This sermon is identical to the expository sermon.

7. The *synthetic sermon* is when the order of the points is rearranged so that they are not in a similar position in the text. In this method, the preacher says not what

is expressed in the text in so many words but what is implied.

8. The *historical sermon* is one in which the points of the sermon treat the material in the past tense.

9. The *contemporary sermon* is one that translates the material into current significance and lists the points in the present tense.

10. The *ethical discourse* (sermon) is taken from a specific Bible passage that directs an ethical message to the believer. The purpose of the sermon is to build Bible morality into the members of the congregation. This particular sermon may not be expository in nature. The textual sermon, in contrast, is expository in nature.

11. The *allegorical sermon* takes certain Bible narratives and gives them an allegorical interpretation.

12. The *biographical sermon* presents a study of the life of a particular Bible character. The facts about the particular character form the basis for a message that has modern application. The biographical sermon can be handled in an expository manner.

13. In the *dramatic monologue* sermon, the preacher becomes the character he or she seeks to present and actually acts out the message of the character.

THE PREACHER'S AUTHORITY

In the area of speech communication, gospel preachers have an advantage that separates them from all other public communicators. There is an ingredient that enables preachers with authority; their words become pointed, sharp, and powerful. The key ingredient—anointed preaching—distinguishes gospel preaching from all other methods of communication. Anointed preaching places God into the sermon and on the preacher. When preachers preach in the power of God, the results are remarkable. They preach with inspiration and fullness of thought. There is both freedom and simplicity of utterance. The results are nothing short of miraculous. This element of the divine in preaching must be foremost in preachers' preparation and delivery if they are to be lastingly effective.

What is this sacred anointing? It is a "divine afflatus" that drives preachers to the point where they have so surrendered themselves to the dynamic of God's power that they are driven along as they proclaim the message. It means to approach preaching as a science or a craft and to risk distancing oneself from the *charisma* (Greek), which refers to the gift by grace distributed to the church by the Holy Spirit. Our salvation is described as the charisma of God (Rom. 5:15).

In the act of preaching, there must be the unknown, vulnerable element that leaves the preacher at the mercy of the Lord's Spirit. The Holy Ghost then takes over, and the result is anointed preaching. The preacher must always have the consciousness of divine power and authority. The minister's call and the urgency of his or her character accent his or her authority. This observation is validated in the history of preaching from the prophets to the modern age.

The authority of the preacher is further strengthened by loyalty to the work of the ministry. Many preachers become engrossed in so many things that their ministries cease to be their major interest. It is very difficult for preachers to engage in full-time business ventures, modern politics, and other absorbing engagements and still hold to the ministry as the supreme purpose and demand of their lives. Such engagements are likely to develop into luke-warmness and the submerging of the passion for preaching. The preaching must constantly deepen the preachers' spiritual lives, widen their social horizons, and lift higher their visions of eternal life in Christ.

There are certain personal moral qualities that are basic in the character of the person called to preach. They may be regarded as reasonable evidence of a person's fitness for the ministerial office.

1. Preachers must have a sense of *divine calling*. It is not something one chooses to do. Therefore, ministers must accept this recognition with appropriate humility and a high sense of responsibility. They must never regard it merely as a mark of personal honor but as an honor to the one who first called people to be ministers.

2. Preachers should have a *vital Christian experience* with the Lord. In addition, preachers should have a call to discipleship—learner, follower, and servant. Their high calling and sense of responsibility demand

that they seek—by earnest prayer, spiritual devotion, and a committed life—a special measure of divine aid and strength to walk circumspectly before the world. Sobriety, moral strength, ethical insight, and spiritual power are required of them. They must have a vital Christian experience with the Lord to be a positive example to those they minister.

3. Effective preachers must *grow in knowledge and understanding.* It is part of the preacher's calling. They who are to exercise the sacred office of interpreter of life and religion in these days must be careful disciples. If they are thus equipped, they will be saved from hasty judgments and opinions that have no solid basis in facts. They must learn to live at the crossroads where the areas of knowledge meet, relating them to the problems of living.

4. Effective preachers will have to *work to develop a natural talent.* Develop your talent, develop your style, and be yourself. All preachers owes themselves strength of character and good reputation. As preachers stands before the people, they must be bigger than themselves. "In the cross of Christ I glory" is always the attitude of appropriate humility. Preachers must be unselfish. They must be of broad sympathies and understanding. All these things will make the preachers' talent natural. They will not be fakes.

5. *Good physical health* is essential to an effective ministry. Several essentials are necessary for the preacher's good health: fresh air, exercise, good food, and rest. You will be able to think more clearly and find that your creative powers are heightened. You cannot engage every preaching opportunity. You must balance your life.

Listen to God—if you need rest, then rest. Otherwise, you will damage your health, lose effectiveness as a minister, or have trouble getting along with others due to stress.

6. An effective preacher will have *complete dependence upon the Holy Spirit.* Pray that God will use you, and pray that God will speak through you. Daily time for Bible study and prayer is essential. We must have strength that can only come from God. Hence, such needed strength is derived from Bible study and prayer (knee-ology and theology). The preacher will benefit from a broad, general education. The study of psychology, history, biology, and sociology would be of great benefit. The preacher should study Hebrew, Greek, Greek syntax, and word origins. The preacher should be trained in theology (both systematic and biblical). Systematic theology has value in that the preacher is given a framework for understanding Bible doctrine. Biblical theology will make preachers aware that they are dealing with the very mind of God in the scriptures. Also, biblical theology will help preachers avoid the danger of putting all Bible doctrine in neat little compartments. Formal study in the area of Bible interpretation is helpful. As preachers learn proper principles of scripture interpretation, they will learn to avoid off-the-wall interpretations. It will make preachers aware of the different interpretations offered for controversial passages. Preachers' holy work can dull their awareness of the need to be alone with God in their personal lives. The need to develop a sense of dependence upon God should not be minimized. We must have the strength that can come only from God.

Such needed strength is derived as we wait before him on our knees, praying the scriptures.

Preaching is effective only when it is accompanied by the Holy Spirit's power. In preaching, actually two are involved, for there must be cooperation between the Spirit of God and the minister of God. An awareness of this partnership brings about confidence and assurance as the preacher stands to preach. The same power that anointed the preachers of the New Testament is at the beckoning of every sincere preacher of the gospel. Preachers need only open themselves to the anointing of the Holy Spirit for preaching power.

The one called to preach must bear the burden of announcing God's redemptive word, whereby sinful individuals will be moved by God's Spirit to remember his loving kindness toward them, to repent of their defiance of his will, and to resolve to live new lives based on his justice and his mercy. If this message has been of any help in understanding the call to preach, then my efforts have not been in vain—to God be the glory! Amen.

Woe is unto me, if I preach not the gospel!

—1 Corinthians 9:16

ENDNOTES

Part 1: The Call to Preach

1 Ralph G. Turnbull, *A Minister's Obstacles* (New York: Fleming H. Revell Co., 1946), 13.
2 Turnbull, *A Minister's Obstacles*, 12.
3 Charles R. Brown, *The Making of a Minister* (New York: The Century Co., 1927), 33.
4 Finis Jennings Dake, *Dake's Annotated Reference Bible* (Lawrenceville, GA: Dake's Bible Sales, 1982), 231.
5 Arthur S. Hoyt, *Vital Elements of Preaching* (New York: The Macmillan Co., 1914), 3.
6 Paul L. Stagg, *What Is the Church?*, ed. Duke K. McCall (Nashville: Boardman Press, 1958), 148–163.
7 J. Spencer Kennard, *Psychic Power in Preaching* (Philadelphia: George W. Jacobs & Co., 1901), xii–xiii.
8 T. W. Manson, *The Church Ministry* (Philadelphia: Westminster Press, 1948), 31–42.
9 John A. T. Robinson, *The Body, A Study in Pauline Theology* (Chicago: Henry Regnery Co., 1952).
10 Morris Ashcraft, "Paul's Understanding of Apostleship," *Review and Expositor* LV (October 1958): 400–412.
11 Page H. Kelly, *Exodus: Called for Redemptive Mission* (Nashville: Convention Press, 1977), 19–23.
12 John A. Broadus, *Lectures on the History of Preaching* (New York: Sheldon & Company, 1876), 14–15.
13 Otto J. Baab, *Prophetic Preaching: A New Approach* (New York: Abingdon Press, 1958), 15–16.

14 Anne Davis and Wade Rowatt Jr., *Formation for Christian Ministry*, 3rd ed. (Louisville: Review and Expositor Press, 1988). From Frank Stagg, "Understanding Call to Ministry," 42.

15 Frank Stagg, *Polarities of Man's Existence in Biblical Perspective* (Philadelphia: Westminster Press, 1973). See especially chapter 2, "Aspective Yet Holistic" and chapter 3, "Individual Yet Corporate," 45–95.

Part 2: Prophecy and Preaching

1 Bernard W. Anderson, *Understanding the Old Testament*, 3rd ed. (Englewood Cliffs, NJ: Prentice-Hall, Inc., 1975), 228. "The Background of Prophecy"—Apparently, the Hebrew word *nabi* is related to the Akkadian *nabu*, which means "to call, announce." There is some uncertainty, however, as to whether the Hebrew has an active meaning ("caller," "announcer") or a passage meaning ("one who is called"). In either case, the word points to the prophet's role as the messenger of God.

2 Claus Westermann, *Basic Forms of Prophetic Speech,* trans. Hugh K. White (Philadelphia: Westminster, 1967), 70–91. This is discussed by Claus Westermann in his analysis of the basic forms of prophetic speech.

3 Abraham J. Herschel, *The Prophets* (New York: Harper & Row, 1963), chapter 1.

4 World's Greatest Bible Scholars, *The System Bible Study* (Kansas City: The System Bible Company, 1949), 265.

5 F. F. Bruce, D. Guthrie, A. R. Millard, J. J. Packer, and D. J. Wiseman, *New Bible Dictionary*, 2nd ed. (Downers Grove, IL: Inter-Varsity Press, 1993), 975.

6 Otto J. Babb, *Prophetic Preaching: A New Approach* (New York: Abingdon Press, 1958), 135.

7 Bernhard W. Anderson, *Understanding the Old Testament* (Englewood Cliffs, NJ: Prentice-Hall, Inc., 1975), 229–230.

8 World's Greatest Bible Scholars, *The System Bible Study*, 265.

9 John A. Broadus, *History of Preaching* (New York: Sheldon & Co., 1876), 13.

10 Leslie J. Tizard, *Preaching: The Art of Communication* (New York: Oxford University Press, 1959), 11–13.

11 John R. Claypool, *The Preaching Event: The Lyman Beecher Lectures* (New York: Harper Collins Publishers, 1989).

12 Gardner C. Taylor, *How Shall They Preach: The Lyman Beecher Lectures and Five Lenten Sermons* (Elgin, IL: Progressive Baptist Publishing House, 1977).

13 John H. C. Fritz, *The Preacher's Manual: A Study in Homiletics* (St. Louis: Concordia Publishing House, 1941).

14 Geoffrey W. Bromily and Donald E. Daniels, *Homiletics: Karl Barth* (Louisville: Westminster/John Knox Press, 1991).

15 Henry H. Mitchell, *Black Preaching: The Recovery of a Powerful Art* (San Francisco: Harper & Row Publishers, 1991).

Part 3: Preachers and Preaching

1 Sidney Greidnanus, *The Modern Preacher and the Ancient Text* (Grand Rapids, MI: Wm. B. Eerdmans Pub. Co., 1988), 7.

BIBLIOGRAPHY

Anderson, Bernard W. *Understanding the Old Testament*, Englewood Cliffs, NJ: Prentice-Hall, Inc., 1975.

Ashcraft, Morris. *Review and Expositor* LV (October 1958).

Baab, Otto J. *Prophetic Preaching: A New Approach.* New York: Abingdon Press, 1958.

Broadus, John A. *Lectures on the History of Preaching.* New York: Sheldon & Company, 1876.

Bromily, Geoffrey W. and Donald E. Daniels. *Homiletics: Karl Barth.* Louisville: John Knox Press, 1991.

Brown, Charles R. *The Making of a Minister.* New York: The Century Co., 1977.

Bruce, F. F., D. Guthrie, A. R. Millard, J. I. Packer, and D. J. Wiseman. *New Bible Dictionary.* 2nd ed. Downers Grove, IL: Inter-Varsity Press, 1993.

Claypool, John R. *The Preaching Event: The Lyman Beecher Lectures.* New York: Harper Collins Publishers, 1989.

Dake, Finis Jennings. *Dake's Annotated Reference Bible*. Lawrenceville, GA: Dake's Bible Sales, 1982.

Davis, A. and W. Rowatt, Jr. *Formation for Christian Ministry*. 3rd ed. Louisville: Review and Expositor Press, 1988.

Fritz, John H. D. *The Preacher's Manual: A Study in Homiletics*. St. Louis: Concordia Publishing House, 1941.

Greidnanus, Sidney. *The Modern Preacher and the Ancient Text*. Grand Rapids, MI: Wm. B. Eerdmans Publishing Company, 1988.

Herschel, Abraham J. *The Prophets*. New York: Harper & Row Publishers, 1963.

Hoyt, Arthur S. *Vital Elements of Preaching*. New York: The Macmillan Co., 1914.

Kelly, Page H. *Exodus: Called for Redemptive Mission*. Nashville: Convention Press, 1948.

Kennard, J. Spencer. *Psychic Powers in Preaching*. Philadelphia: George W. Jacobs & Co., 1901.

Manson, T. W. *The Church Ministry*. Philadelphia: Westminster Press, 1948.

Mitchell, Henry H. *Black Preaching: The Recovery of a Powerful Art*. San Francisco: Harper & Row, Publishers, 1991.

Robinson, John A. T. *The Body: A Study in Pauline Theology*. Chicago: Henry Regnery Co., 1952.

Stagg, Frank. *Polarities of Man's Existence in Biblical Perspective*. Philadelphia: Westminster Press, 1973.

Staff, Paul L. *What Is the Church?* Edited by Duke K. McCall. Nashville: Broadman Press, 1958.

Taylor, Gardner C. *How Shall They Preach: The Lyman Beecher Lectures and Five Lenten Sermons*. Elgin, IL: Progressive Baptist Publishing House, 1977.

Tizard, Leslie J. *Preaching: The Art of Communication*. New York: Oxford University Press, 1959.

Turnbull, Ralph G. *A Minister's Obstacles*. New York: Fleming H. Revell Co., 1946.

Westermann, Claus. *Basic Forms of Prophetic Speech*. Translated by Hugh K. White. Philadelphia: Westminster Press, 1967.

Banks, Edward J., et al. *The System Bible Study*. Kansas City: The System Bible Company, 1949.

ABOUT THE AUTHOR

Dr. Lowell Hardy is a licensed and ordained minister, and he has six degrees, including a doctor of practical theology degree from Master's International School of Divinity in Evansville, Indiana. Dr. Lowell has served in the ministry since 1994, and he remains active in the ministry as an evangelist at various churches. Before joining the ministry, he served in the US Marine Corps and Air Force Reserve during the Vietnam and Persian Gulf Wars, respectively, and he also worked as an electronics technician and as an educator. Today he lives in Garner, North Carolina, with his wife, Portia.